the pop classics series

#1 *It Doesn't Suck.*

Showgirls

#2 *Raise Some Shell.*

Teenage Mutant Ninja Turtles

#3 *Wrapped in Plastic.*

Twin Peaks

#4 *Elvis Is King.*

Costello's My Aim Is True

#5 *National Treasure.*

Nicolas Cage

#6 *In My Humble Opinion.*

My So-Called Life

#7 *Gentlemen of the Shade.*

My Own Private Idaho

gentlemen of the shade. my own private idaho jen sookfong lee

ecwpress

Copyright © Jen Sookfong Lee, 2017

Published by ECW Press
665 Gerrard Street East
Toronto, Ontario, Canada M4M 1Y2
416-694-3348 / info@ecwpress.com

Editors for the press:
Jennifer Knoch and Crissy Calhoun
Cover and text design: David Gee
Series proofreader: Avril McMeekin

Library and Archives Canada
Cataloguing in Publication

Lee, Jen Sookfong, author
Gentlemen of the shade : My own private
Idaho / Jen Sookfong Lee.

(Pop classics ; 7)
Issued also in electronic formats.
ISBN 978-1-77041-313-9 (paperback)
978-1-77305-042-3 (pdf)
978-1-77305-041-6 (epub)

1. My own private Idaho (Motion picture).
2. My own private Idaho (Motion picture)–
Influence. 3. Gay men in motion pictures.
4. Van Sant, Gus–Criticism and
interpretation. 5. Shakespeare, William,
1564-1616–Film adaptations. I. Title.
II. Series: Pop classic series ; 7

PN1997.M926L44 2017   791.43'72
C2016-906418-2   C2016-906419-0

Printing: Webcom   5   4   3   2   1
PRINTED AND BOUND IN CANADA

The publication of *Gentlemen of the Shade* has been generously supported by the Government
of Canada through the Canada Book Fund. *Ce livre est financé en partie par le gouvernement
du Canada.* We also acknowledge the contribution of the Government of Ontario through the
Ontario Book Publishing Tax Credit and the Ontario Media Development Corporation.

MIX
Paper from
responsible sources
FSC® C004071

For Sandra Ka Hon Chu

Contents

Introduction   1

It Was 1991   7

We're Stuck Here Together   19

It Depends on What You Call Normal   39

The Medium Is the Message   57

The Afterlife of Mike and Scott   63

Epilogue   81

Sources   85

Acknowledgments   89

Introduction

In the fall of 1991, when *My Own Private Idaho* was released, I was 15 years old. I had just bought my first pair of Doc Martens (three holes with steel toes) and a batik dress printed with crescent moons. My best friend, Sandra, and I spent every Friday afternoon at the local record store, flipping through the cassettes in the alternative and independent sections, looking for bands we recognized from the university radio station. At school, we sat on the floor, backs against our lockers, whispering about the other students, how they *just didn't get it* and were *so square it was tragic*. If someone had asked us what exactly the other kids didn't get, we probably wouldn't have been able to articulate it. All we knew was that we weren't like them. They wore Guess jeans and hoop earrings and listened to Bell Biv Devoe. They were groomed and smoothly beautiful and smelled like vanilla.

We wanted to be different. And our effort was palpable.

Sandra and I had first heard about *My Own Private Idaho* in *Interview*, in which Gini Sikes and Paige Powell had published an interview, accompanied by a series of appropriately brooding photographs by Bruce Weber of the film's two leads, River Phoenix and Keanu Reeves. Sandra was in love with River, who played the fragile drifter Mike, and who would die two years after the film's release. I was in love with Keanu, who played the handsome, Shakespeare-quoting Scott, and who would go on to blockbuster success in *Speed* and *The Matrix*. We had seen almost all of their previous movies: *Parenthood*, *Running on Empty*, *Bill and Ted's Excellent Adventure*, *Stand by Me*. Both actors were baby-faced, beautiful, soft-spoken in public, and still awkward in their adult bodies. We had never met boys like them anywhere — not at school, not at our summer jobs, not walking through the mall. The photographs in *Interview* were beautiful and relentlessly urban, with both actors seemingly unstyled and unposed, smoking cigarettes in dimly lit rooms in clothes that made it look as if they had fallen asleep in a trashed hotel room and stumbled directly to the photo shoot. But it was what they said that drew us to this weird little movie they had just made together.

I was introduced to so many elements through the guy I was playing. Real people. My imagination. Gus's interpretation. Shakespeare. It was rich! And it was just bottomless, man.

Gus just has those qualities that we all need to get back. Open eyes, open ears, a kid's stream of consciousness.

I have really strong feelings about the search for home and mother.

Clearly, River Phoenix and Keanu Reeves cared deeply about this film, loved making it, loved the end result. It was important to them. Yes, we had to see *My Own Private Idaho*, no matter what.

The week the movie came to Vancouver, we skipped school, took a bus downtown, and settled into a half-empty theater with a group of what appeared to be women in their 70s on a post-lunch outing. We knew almost nothing about the film. The reviews we had read talked about hustlers (a term we could only hazily define), *Henry IV*, sexual identity, and homelessness, but these words meant very little to either of us. We were, after all, only 15, and our worlds were bordered by school, network television, magazines, and radio. As much as we wanted to look different and do different things from the other adolescents around us, we were still very much immersed in popular culture. It was hard to ignore *Beverly Hills, 90210* and Color Me Badd. We watched MuchMusic, Canada's version of MTV, every single day. We cared about the torrid love affair between Julia Roberts and Jason Patric. And so, when we sat in the darkened theater waiting for *My Own Private Idaho* to start, how subversive or different the film might be was only an amorphous thought, as unshaped as our own fumbling grasps at what we understood to be alternative culture.

The movie began. We were in Idaho. Then Seattle. Then Portland. We were watching Mike beg for money from a john. We were in a Chinese diner, and then a porn shop, listening to conversations about sex, bad dates, risk, and money. We followed Mike and Scott to Rome, where the hustlers and johns were eerily similar to their American counterparts.

By the end of the first half hour, four of the older women

had left the theater, seemingly offended. But Sandra and I stayed, fascinated by how these characters — each of them wrapped up in their childhoods and old decisions that no one else could ever really understand — were running through life, eating up beauty and violence, sex and fraternity, drugs and fried noodles. As if this was the way it was supposed to be. As if nice houses and big cars and universities were to be mocked or, even better, totally ignored. As if everything we knew as young women who grew up in a respectable working-class neighborhood where immigrant families passed arugula and bok choy over backyard fences was just a barrier to real life, one that was defined by motorcycles and cheap whiskey and the freedom of wide open, street-centered days.

It was absurd. It was life and death. It was subversive. It shocked us but comforted us too. It was nothing that we could have ever expected. And it would start us on a decade-long adventure, one that prompted us to question the television shows and music and fashion we had been consuming and look for alternatives that were imperfect, that might fail in execution but whose effort we could admire. In 1991, we began to want culture produced by individuals we could identify, individuals who looked like people we might know. We began to ignore the all-boy singing groups that dominated Top 40 radio with their impossibly beautiful skin and jawlines and voices. We began to scour the free alternative newspaper for concerts and art shows and sex advice. I know this is a cliché, but *My Own Private Idaho* was exactly the right movie at the right time. It was the beginning of grunge and the beginning of something much more personal. Sandra and I had just started to construct our own identities, collecting bits and pieces from the world around us and trying them on. *My Own Private Idaho* was one of the first of these bits. And it fit. Just right.

Writer and director Gus Van Sant couldn't have known that his third feature was going to be so pivotal to 1990s culture and the decades afterward, but as the characters stumbled from Idaho to Portland to Rome and back again, their story felt like the very first subversion we understood. They made choices that weren't about finding the right university so they could get the right job and buy the right house in the right neighborhood. They made choices that were soaked with risk but also possibility and believed that being different was better than being good. They lived on the margins of the visible world: they slept on rooftops while others hurried to work, skulked in shadows until a john stopped to pick them up. They veered from experience to experience and cobbled together makeshift identities. This story came to us, to movie theaters that played matinees for teenaged girls who had skipped school. Instead of exploring the margins by leaving the mainstream behind, Gus Van Sant delivered the margins right into our mainstream lives.

When the final credits flashed green and blue, all of our nascent feelings about marginalism, the cult of the alternative, and how art can be both a balm and an excuse had been crystallized on this movie screen, in this theater, before our very eyes. The house lights turned on. We blinked at each other. We would never be the same.

1

It Was 1991

I'VE BEEN TASTING ROADS MY WHOLE LIFE.

I had always thought of the 1990s as a very particular time, as an era when our views of the world and our individual positions in it were constantly shifting, and what we learned in the 1980s about capitalism, HIV/AIDS, sexuality, and diversity was being challenged and rebuilt. But I'm also aware that I'm looking backward through a thick layer of nostalgia. I graduated high school in 1994 and finished university in 1998. I fell in love in 1995 and again in 1997. I wrote a sonnet for the skinny and awkward Beck and, in a fit of obsessive optimism, sent it. (If you're wondering, he still hasn't replied.) It was the decade of my adolescence and young adulthood, and my friends and I changed in many huge ways and many small ways. It was possible that I was confusing these individual changes with global, social ones. After all, no one is more narcissistic than a gloomy 19-year-old writing love poems for famous musicians. And it's not just me: the internet has ballooned with people in midlife writing about their young adulthoods, about that time they saw Jane's Addiction in a 150-seat venue accessible by a stairwell set deep into a Boston alley. The creative output inspired by the 1990s — in film, television, and books — is just beginning. Think of *Fresh Off the Boat*, *Straight Outta Compton*, the explosion of grunge-inspired fashion at Urban Outfitters. The 1990s might have had far less influence than I, or anyone else my age, could objectively measure in 2017.

But as I thought deeper, I came to understand that 1991, when *My Own Private Idaho* was released, was a year full of opposition, drama, banality, and tragedy. Paul Bernardo murdered Leslie Mahaffy. *Generation X* by Douglas Coupland was published. The Gulf War. *Full House*. The conflicts and contradictions were everywhere. You just had to know where to look.

The 1990s were years that produced huge cultural changes, shifts in popular thinking that would shape the trajectory of politics, relationships, and social constructs for the next two decades. Without the 1990s and how it shone a light on outsiders and the culture they were producing as well as consuming, so much of what we've created since then as writers or filmmakers or musicians would not exist. And our intimate lives — whom we sleep with and how openly we do it — would have looked very different. After all, without RuPaul or *Fall on Your Knees* by Ann-Marie MacDonald, we wouldn't have the same tools we have today to discuss or even acknowledge the spectrum of gender and sexuality. *My Own Private Idaho*, released in September of 1991, was one of the harbingers of this sea change. From its visuals to its lead actors to the lo-fi titles that flash between scenes, Gus Van Sant's film is a cinematic fortune cookie: it gave us, an audience who was already dissatisfied with mainstream culture, a beautifully (yet still messily) wrapped narrative that helped shape our forming sensibilities, whether we knew it yet or not.

SHINY, HAPPY PEOPLE

It was tough to deny: if you were living in the Western world, you could easily be lulled into cultural and political complacency. And a large part of this privileged blindness had to do with the power of majority culture. In a review of *My Own Private Idaho* published in *The Washington Post*, Desson Howe likens the film to the ringing of wind chimes, an unimportant sound to some. He writes, "Those with ears to hear will love this music." It was those of us with ears attuned to other, less obvious frequencies who were more than ready for Gus Van Sant's music.

In order to understand the firm grasp majority culture had on the world, we have to remember that our engagement with culture was entirely different in 1991. This was before the internet gave voice to oddity. Writers of fan fiction had a hard time finding each other. Cosplay partners were few and far between. You couldn't pull out your phone and find a BDSM hook-up in five swipes. By necessity, a large portion of the world was watching or listening to or wearing the same things. We talked about *Seinfeld* on Friday mornings because we all had the same cable television subscription. We read *Rolling Stone* to find out which musicians we needed to pay attention to because that was the only popular music magazine available at every corner store. We all wore the same floral dress with the denim jacket from The Gap, the coolest mall store that wasn't cool at all. The idea that the United States was exporting a kind of cultural colonialism with its domination of entertainment was starting to take shape. Bill Clinton, the U.S. president who was famous for his flawless speech delivery and saxophone playing, became a high-profile symbol of American cultural polish when he was elected in 1993. Everything seemed shiny and easy and happy, but, tellingly, only two years into his presidency, he would begin his affair with Monica Lewinsky, the relationship that finally cracked his smooth public façade.

Before Bill Clinton, other realities were emerging to mark 1991. Conflicts were simmering in Rwanda and the former Yugoslavia. Rodney King was beaten by police officers in Los Angeles. In South Africa, it was the end of apartheid. Freddie Mercury openly died from complications of AIDS. If you were the sort to pay attention to the undersides of things, to the ringing of wind chimes, as it were, you noticed. In Vancouver, where I grew up, women from the impoverished and ghettoized Downtown Eastside were disappearing. When I accompanied my mother to Chinatown, which is part of the same neighborhood, I was morbidly fascinated by the women who stood on street corners while I was carrying plastic bags of oranges and barbecued pork. When I passed them on the sidewalks and looked at their faces, they weren't so different from me. Some of them were the same age or listened to the same music or wore the same shade of lipstick. It was one of the few times that the gloss of the early 1990s cracked in my everyday life. In 2007, Robert Pickton would be convicted of murdering six of these women and charged with the murders of 20 more.

There was an abundance of hypocrisy in the world around us. Before *My Own Private Idaho*, I was only dimly aware that this was true and was still, at least partially, a believer in the prettiness of the culture I had grown up in. After *My Own Private Idaho*? That was a whole different story.

WHEN GRUNGE HAPPENED

No discussion about culture in 1991 would be complete without Nirvana and Kurt Cobain. *Nevermind*, the album that catapulted the band to mainstream success, was released on September 24, just three days before *My Own Private Idaho* had its theatrical release in North America. In retrospect, it seems serendipitous.

Recently, I watched the documentary *Kurt Cobain: Montage of Heck*, written and directed by Brett Morgen and co–executive produced by Frances Bean Cobain, Kurt's daughter with Courtney Love. Through journals and drawings, I very distinctly saw and felt Kurt Cobain's pain at living his adolescence in an inhospitable world. With divorced parents, he lived in a series of homes, never really settling with either parent or his extended family. He had difficulty with his peers until he found a community of punk musicians, which eventually led to the formation of Nirvana.

My first exposure to *Nevermind*'s first single, "Smells Like Teen Spirit," was watching the video on MuchMusic, a channel I watched every day for several hours as my main lifeline to popular culture. The song's title, taken from a commercial for a brand of deodorant marketed to youth, seemed innocuous. After all, so much of what we were watching or reading was so suffused with advertising that slogans became as much a part of culture as the television shows or magazine articles themselves. In the "Smells Like Teen Spirit" video, though, there were many signifiers of subversion: the dimly lit high school gym, the kids forming a mosh pit on the hardwood floor, the janitor dancing with his mop, the first few low, moody guitar chords. But for me, it was the cheerleaders in their black uniforms with the red anarchy symbol on their chests — purposely reminiscent of the letter A that Hester Prynne is forced to wear as an adulteress in *The Scarlet Letter* by Nathaniel Hawthorne — that were the most striking. They were both sexy and forbidding, and they wore, proudly, a symbol of anarchy, the most defiant and subversive act of rebellion I had ever seen in popular music. It was sex positive. It was unruly. It was a song and video that changed mainstream music.

Nirvana was the band that didn't just scratch at the surface of the 1990s, it seemed to explode from underneath, like a volcano spitting disenchantment and dirty hair. I could liken it to the emergence of punk in England in the 1970s, or the birth of rock 'n' roll in America in the 1950s, and those examples would both be relevant. But what the 1970s and 1950s didn't have was the high sheen of corporate perfection that characterized so much of the culture we were consuming in 1991. The boys on *Home Improvement* were teeth-achingly cute. Boyz II Men sang crystal clear harmonies. Even *Terminator 2: Judgment Day*, a movie that had a human-led rebellion at its core, generated the most discussion around the new, seemingly psychopathic killing machine played by Robert Patrick, whose liquid metal body was shiny and smooth and, of course, perfect. Nirvana, and especially Kurt Cobain, was decidedly imperfect. Kurt's vocals cracked when he sang high notes. They had formed a three-piece band that sometimes played harder than it played well. When they accepted Best New Artist at the MTV Video Music Awards (presented, incidentally, by Boyz II Men and the also perfect-sounding Wilson Phillips, which made for an awkward moment of 1990s pop culture opposition), Kurt, Krist Novoselic, and Dave Grohl, all with uncombed hair and ill-fitting clothes, seemed pleased, but they also didn't seem to know how to express joy in this mainstream marker of success. Kurt, after thanking Nirvana's "true fans," said quietly, "You know, it's really hard to believe what you read." And then, like the charismatic lead singer of a hugely famous rock band, which he was, he smiled cheekily at the audience and walked off, trophy held closely to his body.

It didn't really matter what you thought of their music. There was no denying their impact on a Western world that had become forebodingly homogenous.

The same world that was ready for Nirvana was ready for *My Own Private Idaho* and, by extension, for culture from the margins that didn't care about perfection, or even quality. The culture that would eventually dominate the 1990s circled around authenticity, perspective, and, above all else, singularity, even if that singularity included missteps and artlessness. How many times did I have a conversation with my friends ridiculing the "posers" who only discovered Pearl Jam after they played *Saturday Night Live* in 1992? How meanly did I laugh at New Kids on the Block when the band tried to grow up and changed its name to NKOTB in 1993?

It wouldn't take long for the high shine of the early 1990s to wear off. Pretty soon, even Bill Clinton couldn't hide the mistakes — the Rwandan Genocide, the Defense of Marriage Act, NAFTA — his administration would make. Pretty soon, the disenchantment I was just beginning to feel on that October afternoon in a dark movie theater would be articulated in every kind of media, from every kind of artist. Banksy began his street art in 1990. David Foster Wallace began writing his sprawling, messy novel *Infinite Jest* in 1991. It's not a coincidence that the popular documentary series VH1's *Behind the Music* premiered in 1997. By then, we were well aware that the version of culture that movie and music producers had been selling to us throughout the decade was designed for easy watching and easy listening. Consumers of culture were developing a taste for mashed-up, undiluted creativity, especially if it included the addictions, the pressures to succeed, and how public scrutiny destroyed fragile egos. They wanted to know that their own lives weren't the only ones that were filled with mistakes and unreliable emotions and fear. The perfection of Mariah Carey was alienating and impossible. And so we pushed back and made antiheroes into real heroes, whether any of them liked it or not.

IF NOT X, THEN WHAT?

In the 1990s, two Canadian books attempted to define generational shifts in opposing genres: *Generation X*, the novel by Douglas Coupland, and *Boom, Bust & Echo*, the business book about economic demography by David K. Foot. When I worked at a bookstore in the mid-1990s, I saw both books selling in huge numbers to all sorts of people — older baby boomers, younger Generation Xers, people in suits trying to understand buying habits and social characteristics. As much as *Generation X* seemed to be a handbook for the grunge-obsessed listeners of Nirvana, and as much as *Boom, Bust & Echo* made sense of the economy my friends and I were about to graduate into, definition seemed pointless.

Generation X is commonly defined as the people born after the post–World War Two baby boom, from the 1960s to 1980. My friends and I were born at the tail end, in the late 1970s, and yet the characteristics of what Gen Xers were purported to be never seemed to fit us exactly. Yes, we were overeducated and underemployed, but the basic tenets of overeducation or underemployment seemed quaint. To be angry at these conditions meant that we had once believed education was supposed to be an entry into a practical job, when we had known for years that this was no longer true. My panicky consumer education teacher in high school taught us the magic of compound interest, but also warned that we might not be hired for the jobs we wanted. It meant that we had no expectations for employment because we had already been told, over and over again, that the 40-year career was dead. We were graduating into a recession and an economy that seemed to be ever-shifting and working for companies that expanded and contracted. None of this was a surprise. And so we looked elsewhere for meaning and self-definition.

Douglas Coupland, born in 1961, is 15 years older than me. David Foot, a Harvard graduate and university professor, was well established in academic circles by 1991. Back then, I was a 15-year-old Chinese Canadian girl who wrote poems in the margins of my geometry homework and hung pictures of Jason Patric and Keanu Reeves (clearly, I had a type: dark-haired and moody) in my locker. Even by the end of the 1990s, when I was 23 and trying to write my first novel while working at three part-time jobs, a discussion on my choices or the future of my professional life seemed irrelevant. I was living an adolescence and young adulthood built around flexibility and a willingness to learn new ways of thinking about gender and sexuality and diversity. It was how I learned to pay the rent and form friendships. Definition — the act of writing down the essence of a generation on paper and publishing it in a book — was the exact opposite of the adaptability that had characterized my relationship to the shifting, conflicted world to date. Whatever Douglas Coupland and David Foot were trying to tell me about how most of my generation was going to end up didn't matter. The mainstream was already using them to try and make sense of Generation X — their books were being discussed on daytime television talk shows — and this seemed hopelessly inauthentic. The perfect world we had already chosen to disengage from was clinging to relevancy by adopting our vocabulary in ways that were inaccurate and, well, laughable.

Definition was, even then, something to ridicule. In 1992, the *New York Times* published the much-maligned "Lexicon of Grunge," a glossary of grunge terms given to them, as a prank, by an employee at Sub Pop Records during an interview. Not only were the terms fake, but the very act of trying to define grunge, or alternative culture, was hopelessly structured. Trying to place a generation or a movement into a box in real time was out of step, particularly with this movement, which was marked by its plurality, adaptability, and authenticity. The "Lexicon of Grunge," published in the American newspaper of record for millions of readers to shake their heads over, was the antithesis of all of that.

In 1991, the world was waiting for something real, or at least something that was more real than McRib sandwiches and the sweetly bland songs performed by DJ Jazzy Jeff &

The Fresh Prince. We were teetering on an edge. Behind us was the flawless culture we had grown up in. We were waiting for our authentic, visceral lives to begin, ready, like Mike and Scott, to experience anything and everything we could get our hands on. Literally and figuratively, we sat in a silent theater, waiting for the right movie to start.

2

We're Stuck Here Together

I MEAN FOR ME, I COULD LOVE SOMEONE EVEN IF I, YOU KNOW, WASN'T PAID FOR IT. I LOVE YOU, AND YOU DON'T PAY ME.

Any discussion on the careers and lives of River Phoenix and Keanu Reeves is marked by two things: River Phoenix's drug-induced death in 1993 outside the notorious Los Angeles night club The Viper Room, and Keanu Reeves's improbable success in a series of dark and futuristic action movies, most notably the Matrix trilogy, in which he plays a Messiah-like character who is destined to save humanity. Mythologies have been built around both actors. In death, River Phoenix became a symbol of the excesses of the grunge era, an extension of his character in *My Own Private Idaho*: the wandering, hurting Mike, whose life and body were vulnerable to the caprices of the people and situations around him. The acting success of his brother, Joaquin, who has been nominated for three Academy Awards and has had a publicly fraught relationship with fame and the Hollywood machine, has only added to River's post-death narrative. Keanu Reeves, whose personal life has remained remarkably private for the level of his success, is adored and mocked in equal parts for his acting style, which has developed into a combination of mannered stiffness and rangy physicality. In 2016, the comedy team of Jordan Peele and Keegan-Michael Key wrote and starred in a movie homage, appropriately titled *Keanu* (the title character is a lost kitten). Memes of Sad Keanu photographs proliferate online.

In 1991, however, both actors were just starting to play adult roles. Both had starred in a number of family-oriented mainstream movies: River Phoenix in *Stand by Me* and *Running on Empty*. Keanu Reeves in *Parenthood* and *Bill and Ted's Excellent Adventure*. Back then, there was no public history of drug use, no groundbreaking fight scenes with slow-motion bullets. Back then, River and Keanu were beautiful boys with movie-star hair, who were featured in teen magazines and rode motorcycles, tailed by photographers. These were the young men I recognized. These were the young men I had already fallen in love with. And these were the young men I wanted to see when I bought my ticket for *My Own Private Idaho*.

In Gus Van Sant's previous film, *Drugstore Cowboy*, Matt Dillon (a former teenage idol himself, largely because of his role in the 1983 movie *The Outsiders*, which also starred future heartthrobs Tom Cruise, Patrick Swayze, Rob Lowe, and Emilio Estevez) played the leader of a group of addicts who rob pharmacies to feed their drug habits. *Drugstore Cowboy*, released in 1989, similarly explores alienation, young masculinity, community, and risk, and also uses the fame of its handsome male star for the built-in fanbase while subverting the very notion of stardom or, perhaps more accurately, perfect and youthful beauty.

Matt Dillon is Bob, a young man in 1970s Portland who is addicted to heroin, but who will ingest any drug available to him. With his wife, Dianne, and another couple played by James Le Gros and a very young Heather Graham, he travels around the Pacific Northwest, robbing pharmacies and staying one step ahead of a hapless police detective. As a gang leader, Bob is less a criminal mastermind and more an overgrown, wayward Peter Pan. In an early scene with Kelly Lynch, who plays Dianne, Matt Dillon hunches in an armchair, his forehead wrinkled, and he pushes her half-naked body away, in an effort to plan their next heist without distraction. Her reaction, a combination of sexual frustration, anger, and housewife-like ennui, seems middle-aged, the reaction of a woman who has been stuck alone in her living room all day, taking sips from a gin and tonic. She collapses on the couch and hisses, "You won't fuck me and I always have to drive." In opposition, Matt Dillon plays Bob with an adolescent and slouchy resentment and appears far younger than his on-screen wife. Kelly Lynch is, in fact, five years older than Matt Dillon, and in *Drugstore Cowboy*, this age difference highlights Dianne's flinty commitment to an underground life versus Bob's prettiness and sweetly bumbling burglaries. He might be a career criminal who bounces between a series of seedy apartments, and who drags a dead body down a logging road and into the woods, but he is, visually at least, still a boy, much like Mike in *My Own Private Idaho*. And, in the end, it's Bob who decides to go straight and find a real job "drilling holes in things," proving, perhaps, that he was always the soft-hearted (and soft-featured) one.

Mike and Scott are thematic descendants of Matt Dillon's Bob: he creates his own gang to survive but also to fill his need for companionship in a life where even his mother rejects him. And all three characters are achingly beautiful young men, purposely placed in roles and cinematic worlds that are decidedly the opposite — criminal, seedy, and dangerous.

As Gus Van Sant said in an interview with *Out* magazine in 2015, "[*My Own Private Idaho*] was also a comment on them as boy stars — they were hustling in a different way, for the business." There is nothing lovely or deifying about drug addiction, just as there is nothing deifying about street prostitution. And yet there is no doubt that Van Sant's casting choices were as much about aesthetics as they were about thematic consistency, and that he is, visually, equating a life on the margins with real, lived beauty. The opening shots of *My Own Private Idaho* frame Mike's face as he considers a lonely road in the unrelenting sunshine and then cut to his face again as he's being fellated by a considerably less beautiful and less youthful john. As the film unfolds, both Mike and Scott are positioned in scenes to showcase their beauty. Sometimes, they're still, like in the sex scene between Mike, Scott, and Hans. Sometimes, they're moving, like when Scott is pacing in a grassy, brick-lined alley, explaining to his street mentor, Bob Pigeon, how he will one day leave this life and return to his wealthy and influential family. Yes, Gus Van Sant is creating contrast here, a kind of chiaroscuro effect that brings the ugliness of street life into sharp focus (it's no accident, also, that all the johns in the film are older, odd, or unattractive; beauty, it seems, is reserved for the young and adventurous), but he is also indulging in the beauty of his two lead actors. They are shot and framed carefully, even when Mike is falling into a narcoleptic stupor, even when Scott, in a leather jacket and dog collar, is being scolded by his father.

As beautiful as they looked, the movie made us see that there was more underneath that they were willing to access as actors in order to bring us Mike and Scott.

When they were acting, they were transparent. Neither character filters their thoughts, instead bouncing from city to city while saying what they want, to whomever they want. Mike pretends to choke when a young woman blows cigarette smoke in his face while he's eating. Scott plays with a leather BDSM wrist cuff in public. What we didn't know then was that the lives of Mike and Scott were probably close to how both River and Keanu were living in the early 1990s. In the *Interview* article from November 1991, Keanu arrives for the conversation on a motorcycle and complains about an encounter with paparazzi on his way, saying, "I beat it out of there. It was weird." River, of course, was hiding a deeply serious drug habit and a tendency to disappear into a kind of anti-Hollywood second life where he led an obscure band and lived on a family compound in rural Florida. It's not hard to see the glimmers of who River and Keanu really were in their portrayals of Mike and Scott. Both actors were, at the time, uncomfortable with their teen idol status and used press junkets as a way of dispelling their sweet-faced reputations. When asked about *My Own Private Idaho* hurting his image, Keanu snorted, "Hurt my *image*? Who am I — a politician?"

It was precisely this transparency of character and actor (which comes to a head during the campfire scene, whose dialogue was written by River and Gus Van Sant in collaboration) that allowed us to see the pasts Mike and Scott were carrying: Mike's unstable family and the crushing pressure Scott felt to be just like his father. It gave us the perfect, unobstructed view. We could see that there was more, that there is always more, whether it was contained within a fictional movie and acted by famous young heartthrobs, or contained within our own bodies and manifesting in ways we were just starting to recognize and understand.

TWO GUYS CAN'T LOVE EACH OTHER

When we talk about our moments of sexual awakening (a topic of conversation that seems to crop up every time I have a glass of wine with a group of similarly minded pop culture obsessives), we often talk about scenes from film or television that pulled the sleeping adolescent out of our mostly still childlike bodies. Princess Leia in the gold bikini. Kiefer Sutherland's simmering evilness in *The Lost Boys*. Any number of scenes from *Flashdance*. For me, it was always Mike and Scott, shirtless and in bed together in a decrepit hotel, mocking the city officials and police officers who have been sent to bring Scott home to his family.

Images of gay male sexuality were not totally new to me, but this was the first time I had seen them in a film (*My Own Private Idaho* was many firsts for me: my first independent film, the first R-rated movie I saw without my older sisters, the first reason I skipped school). And it was certainly the first time I had seen young men engaged in sex with each other. Until *My Own Private Idaho*, it had never occurred to me that gay men, whom I had mostly associated with my friend Kate's father and his partner (a pastor and a politician, respectively), were relevant to my sexuality. Seeing Mike and Scott care for each other, hold each other, and then have their relationship end with betrayal was a relationship trajectory I had never considered for gay men, if I had ever considered the relationships of gay men at all.

So, simultaneously, I was turned on by the beauty of Mike and Scott, but I was also turned on by their relationship, which was at once sexual and fraternal and transient. (After all, it's not Mike and Scott's relationship that lasts until the closing scenes, but rather Mike's relationship with the lonely road, a relationship that is really with himself.) And, as all of this was happening in a brain and body that had only just come out of childhood, I was learning about the plurality of sexuality and gender, and about the many ways love, relationships, and heartache can manifest. Scott has a sexual relationship with his street mentor, the Falstaff-like Bob Pigeon, who speaks in Shakespearean lines and loves Scott like a son but also like a partner. Mike's brother is also his biological father. The relationships in *My Own Private Idaho* contain many points of intersection, some positive and others not so positive, and no friendship or family connection is ever just what it seems. Does Bob pay Scott for sex? Does Mike's brother feel abused or loved? Are these contradictions of hurt and loyalty as apparent to the characters as they are to us?

Perhaps the most telling narrative trick is that Gus Van Sant doesn't answer these obvious questions about sex and abuse and power. The characters react by pulling pranks or embarking on extended road trips, but there is no payback, no revenge that soothes the pain that occurs. *Thelma & Louise*, which was also released in 1991, is a road trip movie, one that mines similar territory of relationships gone sour, gender roles, and the primacy of friendship. However, Thelma and Louise are motivated by the men in their lives who have hurt them. We know, without a doubt, that the man who tries to rape Thelma is an awful human being, and he's killed, by Louise, for his transgression. Later, when a trucker harasses the two women on the highway, they shoot up and explode his tanker. Gus Van Sant doles out no such punishment, and the audience is left with the puzzle of how we can love those who hurt us and the infinite number of ways relationships, gay or straight, can unfold.

These lessons — emotional and social — were pivotal. If I could accept that I had sexual feelings for Mike and Scott, two young men who had both straight and gay experiences, and that their complicated relationship made sense for them as individuals and as a couple, then the evolution of how the world would come to understand sexuality and gender in later years was not so difficult for me to navigate. In 1991, seeing this multiplicity after years of flatly perfect mainstream culture felt like a door blowing wide open.

THE TRICK OF AUTHENTICITY

The connection between what we think of as authentic and what exists outside the mainstream can be a tenuous one. After all, there is nothing necessarily less authentic about life in the mainstream or our reactions to it. Just because millions of people, mostly in North America, were watching *Seinfeld* doesn't mean that our engagement with the television series — which played with our ideas of what a sitcom was and how likable the characters should be — was any less real. And today, the authenticity of a film or a musician is less in question. It's very difficult now for an artist to hide behind slick layers of marketing. Audiences demand interaction, whether that's through personal photographs on Instagram or revealing interviews in *Vanity Fair* or shaky video taken on a smartphone and streamed on TMZ.com. Perhaps (or probably) these interactions are also the results of a marketing plan and not authentic at all, but the public perceives them as having some level of real, human exchange.

In 1990, Milli Vanilli, the pop duo of Fab Morvan and Rob Pilatus, was exposed for lip syncing and not providing the vocals on their Grammy-winning album. The Recording Academy stripped the pair of their Best New Artist award. Clearly, Milli Vanilli's cultural product — their music — wasn't authentic. Revoking their Grammy was an outsized act that symbolized what their fans all over the world, and the music industry, felt: duped. While the connection people felt to their music was certainly real, the discovery that this was all fake left a bitter taste in their mouths. Our search, in a sense, for an authentic experience has as much to do with the search for the right authentic product as it does with our emotional and intellectual reactions to that product. We want to believe that what we love and obsess over has been created with as much genuine emotion as it elicits from us. And when we discover that it's not, then we question whether it was worth consuming in the first place. The exchange, in all its aspects, must feel real, even if it really isn't.

In 1991, there was no such exchange in the mainstream. Albums and television shows and movies were presented to us as complete packages. There were, of course, tabloid magazines and entertainment news shows, but there were no celebrity gossip blogs, no Kanye West Twitter feeds to follow. What was mainstream, like *Full House* and Dean Koontz novels, appeared to be delivered to us smoothly and easily. In reality, the creators — the scriptwriters or songwriters or directors

— were hidden by other teams: marketing teams, test audiences, video producers, publicists. The perfection those teams developed and disseminated was at once aspirational and unattainable. And there was no direct line, no direct messages on Instagram, to the creators at all.

This kind of experience was only half-human. Yes, there were humans generating our culture and creating the marketing and delivery systems, but the actual engagement wasn't between two people, but rather between one person and the results of another person's work. And this was obvious. There was no possible way that Whitney Houston's life was that beautiful and that perfect all the time (and it's clear now that it certainly wasn't). No family headed by a single parent was as fun as the Russos on *Blossom*. We were in relationships with publicists and managers as much as we were in relationships with the content they were paid to promote.

So, as I watched *My Own Private Idaho* for the first time, everything about it — from the home movie flashbacks to Mike's childhood, to the disjointed images of spawning salmon and falling barns, to Mike's awkward narcoleptic fits — was surprising and seemed to be designed to jolt us out of our cultural complacency. Some of it was imperfect, like the close-up shots of River Phoenix's face dotted with acne. Some of it was a blunt comment on the grit of the characters' lives, like Scott's father recoiling at his son's stench. When Mike, Scott, and their friends are running from a police raid, they hurtle up an abandoned hotel's crumbling staircase, tripping over dogs and crooked floorboards, and hesitate visibly when they're trying to decide which hallway to turn into. This chase scene isn't crafted for the most narrative impact and isn't choreographed like it would be in a Jean-Claude Van Damme movie. Instead, it's jerkily human — clumsy and without background music. Of course, *My Own Private Idaho* is a crafted and carefully edited film; none of the directorial choices that Gus Van Sant made are by accident and we are, like with more polished cultural products, in a relationship with his film, not with him or his emotions. But the way *My Own Private Idaho* is presented — with the grime of being human on clear display and the oddball yet deliberate cinematic structure — creates, at the very least, the illusion of an interaction that's more intimate, exposing, and, yes, authentic by defying our cultural expectations. In 1991, that was as close as we were going to get to a friendship with Gus Van Sant.

While Mike and Scott are in Snake River, following a trail left by Mike's mother, they run into the ubiquitous Hans, who pays them to have sex with him in a beige and eerily featureless hotel room (where he regales them with a stripped-down version of a musical act he used to perform in Germany, which is equal parts sweet, creepy, and comedy gold). This sex scene is shot as a series of tableaux, with Mike, Scott, and Hans holding still in various positions, naked but sometimes wearing a Mexican wrestler's mask. These are not stills, but shots of the trio holding their positions, visibly breathing. The light is low, and the poses are varied and often surprising. The men are beautiful, of course, but they are also touched with awkwardness, boredom, and kink (nipple clamps make a brief but prominent cameo). This is a scene designed to turn on and unsettle the viewer, but it's also designed to present masculine sexuality in a way that I have always, until now, privately considered to be in direct contrast to the movie *Top Gun*. (I know. Stay with me.)

Top Gun, directed by Tony Scott, was released in 1986 and was a huge commercial hit. In many ways, it's an unremarkable action movie featuring fast planes, alpha males, and a soaring soundtrack (who can forget the hypermasculine "Danger Zone," performed by Kenny Loggins?). Maverick and Ice Man — Tom Cruise and Val Kilmer, respectively — played competing fighter pilots, and their exchanges, full of bravado and a simmering manly rage, are the pinnacle of 1980s bland machismo and the pop culture opposite of River Phoenix's Mike. They spit insults at each other in locker rooms and vie for the attention of women in bars. This is well-trodden territory for the depiction of men in Hollywood action films. But in one specific way, *Top Gun* is very, very memorable.

That beach volleyball scene.

This scene, filled with shirtless student pilots playing an extended, sweaty volleyball game, was what my older sisters and their friends talked about over and over again. Handsome men display their flawless bodies. They wear sunglasses in the bright sunlight. Their chests are shiny and hairless and smooth. They high five each other. They're agile and relentlessly, traditionally masculine.

In *My Own Private Idaho*, Gus Van Sant's decision to treat his pivotal sex scenes as moments of stasis (he does the same when Scott and Carmella fuck in Italy) is a way of saying, "Wait. Consider this. Consider it slowly." The viewer sees every detail in these moments. The positions. The props. The expressions on their still, silent faces. There is no narrative frame, no beginning or middle or end. There is just the sex, the gay male three-way sex. Thematically, this is a challenge to the audience; remember: this is a very frank portrayal of queerness in a film that had a commercial North American release, which was extraordinary for 1991. But it's a narrative challenge as well. The viewer is put into the position of answering basic storytelling questions in order to fill the gaps that Gus Van Sant leaves blank. How does Hans ask them to do this? Do they talk while they have sex? Do Mike and Scott enjoy this, or is it only for money? To me, at 15, this scene felt incisively authentic for our implied participation, its fleshy physicality and polyamory, and for how closely we were challenged to look at and think about men having sex with each other. Gus Van Sant, at the very least, provokes a visceral response. Maybe some people were repelled. Maybe some were aroused. Maybe others were just curious. All of the responses were real, even if the sex we were watching was a cinematic sleight of hand. For a movie, it really doesn't get any more interactive than that.

The perfection of the men in *Top Gun* is beautiful and sexy, of course, but it's also distant. The actors have been groomed and shaved and show no vulnerability or discomfort. We all wonder, for example, how Tom Cruise could play beach volleyball in the blistering sunshine in those stiff 1980s jeans. At the beginning of the 1990s, we had been rendered cynical by the betrayal of Milli Vanilli, which was a double violation of authenticity, one that made us question both the music and our reactions to that music. It didn't take long for *Top Gun* to also seem inauthentic, with its unquestioning patriotism and rigid depictions of oiled and muscled masculinity, and that, in turn, made us wonder if our sexual attachment was grounded in mainstream and commercial illusion. There is nothing real about hot student pilots jumping in the sand in a movie about fighter jets and the hubris of youth. Has anyone ever stumbled upon such a scene in real life while walking the dog? Arguably, there is nothing real about *My Own Private Idaho* either, with its sporadic Shakespearean dialogue and visual fragmentation. But the relationships, and the very imperfect ways Gus Van Sant films the different versions of sex throughout, felt very real to me, partly because of their plurality, but also because the actors played these scenes with humour, desire, and a convincing level of awkwardness. Sex is awkward and sometimes kind of funny. A shirtless Tom Cruise in *Top Gun* is not. Gus Van Sant gave audiences a film that visually and aurally unsettled us, thereby forcing us to consider the structure of his story and the very human, very fragmented trajectory of his characters. He took the mess of life and put it on a screen.

This was, then, an authentic experience within a very mannered, very crafted film. By pushing us toward the margins, toward his street hustlers and the porn shops and the squatters' hotel, Van Sant presented a version of experience that relied on its position in the margins. And he forced us to react, to have real feelings about the scenes we were watching and to engage in a relationship with his film that meant more than the stunned viewership we experienced while watching the shiny spectacle of *Top Gun*. We needed to walk to the edge and teeter there in order to know we were alive.

RISK, ON SCREEN AND OFF

At 15, when I first watched *My Own Private Idaho*, my sexuality was still a fetal idea. But even though there are few women in the film, the experiences of Mike, Scott, and their group of street hustlers carry many of the same ideas of risk that shadow young women as they begin to make decisions for their sexual selves while other aspects of their sexualities are imposed upon them. In one of the early scenes, the young men are eating in a Chinese diner and sharing, to the camera, the stories of their first bad dates with violent johns. Digger, played by Michael Parker, who had, for a time, lived on the street in Portland before acting in a series of Van Sant's movies, recounts how a date ". . . basically raped me, stuck a wine bottle up my butt." They tell their stories flatly, with little emotion, but the pain is there, in their hesitations and how clearly they can remember small details. "There was nothing I could do," Digger says quietly. "We were in the woods, in a thicket."

These are their *first* bad dates. They continue with their street hustling, perhaps because they need money or lack other options. The film never explicitly discusses why any character engages in sex work, but there is an implication that this life, even with the inherent risks, is wide open, that each day can be filled with everything or nothing, and that the focus on lived experience, rather than school or traditional work or obligations, is the real way to understand who we are and what we're meant to be. The young men might be running away from families who were neglectful or abusive or disdainful, but, in between and sometimes during dates, they also have fun. They ride motorcycles, play pranks on each other, shout joyfully from rooftops into the early morning air.

The idea that risk could be acceptable, or that it was an inevitable part of being intensely alive as a whole sexual, physical, and emotional being became an enormous part of how I made intimate and not-so-intimate decisions from 1991 onward. And so it was with Mike, the moral center of *My Own Private Idaho*, with his startling innocence and unprotected heart.

Mike, as written by Gus Van Sant, is a vulnerable, overgrown boy. He collapses unconscious on sidewalks, where he could be robbed or beaten. He has sex with men for money, even though these dates often carry a heavy weight of intimate risk. And he is in love with Scott, who approaches his life with pragmatism and forethought, planning and announcing in advance his departure from the hustler's life. However, even though the role was written by Gus Van Sant, it's also River Phoenix's performance that adds a viscerally childlike layer to Mike and his relationships.

River Phoenix was, by 1991, a critically acclaimed actor for his performances in *Stand by Me* and *Dogfight*, but he was also capable of acting in commercial hits, like *Running on Empty* and *The Mosquito Coast*. By the time he had finished filming *My Own Private Idaho*, at age 20, he had been supporting his entire family with his acting career for eight years, ever since he played the youngest boy in the television remake of *Seven Brides for Seven Brothers*. In many ways, unlike most 20-year-olds, who are still in school or bouncing from one entry-level job to another, he was an adult before his time with an adult-sized load of responsibilities. As Mike, with his clumsily executed jumps and kicks, his awkward expressions of love and joy, there is a distinct hint that River Phoenix, despite living a very grown-up life, was much more a child than his job or family would suggest.

In *Last Night at the Viper Room: River Phoenix and the Hollywood He Left Behind*, author Gavin Edwards offers a theory for River's high-spirited energy in this performance. He grew up on a commune in Venezuela as part of a group called Children of God, whose leader mixed tenets of Christianity, '60s-era counter-culture, and sexual freedom, which included, among other things, the celebration of children as sexual beings. Throughout his life, River Phoenix gave conflicting answers to questions about his childhood, sometimes hinting at sexual abuse, sometimes dismissing the Children of God as no more than a hippie community that his family left for practical reasons. However, what was always a part of his story was that the Phoenix children grew up without formal education, often without outside friends, and were encouraged to perform as buskers or actors from the time they were school age.

It's an easy connection to make that River, who had lacked stability and a childhood free of adult concerns, felt an emotional commonality with Mike, whose own past, with a mother who struggled with her mental health and an older brother simmering with rage, was riddled with neglect and inconsistency. Seemingly, River had experience with growing up before he was ready and understood how Mike's desire for a traditional childhood could manifest in his gangly physicality and his exposed innocence, both voluntary (his willingness to tell Scott how much he loves him, a scene that Gus Van Sant has said was partially written by River) and involuntary (his narcolepsy). Mike wants to experience unfettered, childlike joy, and he does this by never saying no to a prank or spontaneous trip around the world. He allows himself to feel, even if his heart might break, because there's a possibility that it might not. It could end violently or sadly, or it could all end with happiness and love. Like a child, he absorbs experience. Like a hurting adult, he compensates by running headfirst into everything that's offered to him.

These decisions may have been dangerous, and they may have hurt Mike, but like him I was willing to take risks in order to accelerate my understanding of intense emotion and sexual identity. The narrative of sexual education when I was in high school was almost solely focused on diseases and unwanted pregnancies. The idea that sex could be joyful and that I could make that choice seemed like a revelation. Of course, a condom could break. Of course, a partner could exploit my trust and hurt me. All of that could happen. But there could be great rewards too, and this was what I was willing to take risks for. *My Own Private Idaho* would not be the only cultural experience that explored this idea in the 1990s: there was Tori Amos's album *Under the Pink* in 1994, and Marya Hornbacher's *Wasted: A Memoir of Anorexia and Bulimia* in 1998, both of which examine femininity and socially sanctioned ways of expressing female sexuality. However, *My Own Private Idaho* was the first that I understood and the first that communicated one very important idea: that I wasn't the only one worried about my sexual identity and willing to take chances to figure it out.

3

It Depends on What You Call Normal

THE FAMILIES ON THE OTHER SIDE OF THE TRACKS

My Own Private Idaho presents two polar opposites: Mike's family, headed by a mentally ill single mother who struggles with money and boyfriends, and Scott's family, led by his imperious father, the mayor of Portland. The two families, each of them lacking what their sons want and need, drive the story forward. For me, and for most of the film's audience, both of these families exist on the margins. I grew up in an immigrant, working-class family. My parents and grandparents worked hard so that we could own our house, drive a reliable car, and send my sisters and me to university. We weren't poor and we weren't rich, like many North American families. Mike's brother lives in a trailer, drinking cheap whiskey and eating canned dog food. Scott's father has men in suits at his disposal and sits at an oversized, dark wood desk, his salt and pepper hair perfectly arranged. These families — the very, very poor and the very, very rich — were not people we knew.

My Own Private Idaho was always a subversive film, because of both narrative and style, but I think, in some ways, the most subversive thing Gus Van Sant created was a vacuum where the middle class, or the mainstream, could have existed. Structurally, there is no mainstream in his versions of Portland and Seattle. There was trailer park and municipal elite and nothing in between.

There could be a few reasons for this empty space that the middle class usually inhabits. The dominant culture of the 1990s — reflected in television shows like *Step by Step* — was stuffed full of middle class, usually white, families. *My Own Private Idaho* didn't need to show us more Tanners or Taylors. Instead, it brought us two families whose lives were untenable for their sons. For Mike, hustling on the street is preferable to the cauldron of secrets that his brother broods over, and even though he longs for his mother, he also understands that she didn't provide a consistent home for him, either physically or emotionally. It's Scott who nurtures him, and only temporarily. This transience has followed Mike everywhere. His mother took care of him, for a while. His brother is affectionate, until his rage boils over and he becomes violent. Mike, because of his family, expects nothing to be permanent, but longs for it anyway.

For Scott, the street is a reprieve from the pressure of being his father's son. In an early scene, Scott drags an unconscious

Mike to a grassy spot in a wealthy neighborhood. In the night, he delivers a soliloquy (one of the instances where Scott's narrative converges with that of Prince Hal from *Henry IV*) and says,

> I almost get sick thinking that I am a son to him. You know you have to be as good as him to keep up, you have to be able to lift as big a weight, you have to be able to throw that weight as far. Or make as much money. Or be as heartless. To hold your ground. My dad doesn't know that I'm just a kid. He thinks I'm a threat.

The streets are a way for him to ignore a perceived inevitability for his adult life and also to disappoint his father in one spectacular, holistic way. If Scott sleeps on the sidewalk and has sex with men for money, he is deliberately dismantling a set of expectations that he has lived under his whole life. If he had, instead, tried to be the son that his family wants and to be just like his father, his failures might have been less dramatic and shocking, but there would have been further expectations to be better and to try harder. The disappointments might then be constant and accumulate and, in a sense, be heavier and even more intolerable than Scott's disappearance from his privileged life, for both him and his father. If he drops out entirely, then he only needs to survive because, in Jack Favor's mind, the grand, all-encompassing failure has already occurred.

Mike and Scott, though, don't run into an abyss when they escape their respective families. Instead, they run toward Bob Pigeon.

Bob Pigeon is the most Shakespearean of all the characters in *My Own Private Idaho*, which uses lines and other structures from *Henry IV, Part One* and *Part Two*. In *Henry IV*, Prince Hal ignores his royal duties to his father and instead spends his days drinking and carousing with a group of ruffians in a grungy pub before returning to his rightful position as a prince and, later, a king in *Henry V*. The leader of this ragtag gang is Falstaff, a character who, like Hamlet, is a popular topic of study among Shakespeare scholars. Gus Van Sant, who perhaps identified with Falstaff's joyful existence at the fringes of society, used him to develop the Bob Pigeon character, played with loudmouthed glee by William Richert. Like Falstaff, Bob has created his own gang of stray dogs and homeless young people, Mike and Scott included. And like Falstaff, Bob is an exercise in self-myth and self-identity, and the ways in which we define ourselves away from our familial origins and away from the mainstream lives our families often wish for us. Mike's and Scott's families are buried under old truths about incest and expectations. Bob represents the total opposite: instead of enduring his past, he blithely creates his own present and rewrites the past he wishes he had experienced. Why would he wallow in memories when he can build a story that reframes his role from an overweight petty criminal obsessed with younger men into that of a street-wise hero and a fearless leader?

Bob and the young people who squat in *My Own Private Idaho*'s abandoned hotel comprise a constructed family of choice in a film where birth families represent a lack of choice. Mike's life as a hustler seems inevitable. What other kind of life would he live, given his childhood? Scott's life as the heir to his father's political legacy is never his choice either; like Prince Hal, he chooses to live with his gang of homeless friends rather than try to meet his family's expectations and risk failure. This is an outsized, accelerated version of what adulthood means for everyone: we grow up to make choices, we make our own families with friends and lovers, and we develop a familial moral code, even if that moral code includes mugging a rock band on its way home from a gig. It's a classic trope in literature and film: a character feels burdened by family or high school or social conventions and does everything he can to dismantle it and experience something beyond the boundaries that have been pre-determined for him. In the end, he comes to an understanding about his identity and his place in the world and builds a community, or family, to belong to.

Gus Van Sant took this trope and created a fictional family of choice that is both deeply subversive in origins and intimacies and deeply traditional in evolution and structure. Bob's children are sometimes also his lovers. They alternately mock and idolize him. Still, this is a family with a man at its head, a patriarchal leader who makes many of their decisions, who demands respect and usually receives it. And, like all of us, Bob's gang is a product of adolescence and emergent adulthood, of the choices we consciously make that are sometimes compatible with our birth families and sometimes dialectically not. Gus Van Sant's coming-of-age narrative is not characterized by simple or common choices; he gives us the hyperreal version, where we make the riskiest of decisions, and leaves the middle class alone. He has no interest in showing us what would happen if Bob, Mike, and Scott had decided to go to college, get married, and work at a bank.

For 26 years, I thought of *My Own Private Idaho* as being apolitical, as being the kind of movie that is far more concerned with art and character and pushing structural boundaries than it is about any kind of political or social commentary. For the most part, I think this is true, except in the glaring lack of a middle class. There are no restaurant owners, no taxi drivers, no teachers. There are only Jack Favor's lackeys — the assistants and police officers who break down the barricaded door in the abandoned hotel Bob and his gang of street kids have been sleeping in. These men, who wear either dark suits or dark uniforms, are simply employees, sent to do a powerful man's bidding. When examined together, the uniformed worker bees and the missing mainstream point to a deeply political statement, which is that the middle class isn't all that interesting. Or that the middle class has been the subject of more stories than it deserves and that, in 1991, we had had our fill of backyard conversations and cute babies bringing squabbling families together. The year before *My Own Private Idaho*, David Lynch's surreal television series about small town dysfunction, *Twin Peaks*, premiered. Although it only lasted two seasons, the series made an important point about the apparent idyll of the middle class: there was an audience for its opposite, or for depictions of the middle class as long as there was something creepy simmering underneath.

But I think that Gus Van Sant's main intention for leaving

out the mainstream was structural: he didn't need to show us to ourselves. We were already sitting in the audience, engaging with his film. By leaving out stories that we were already familiar with, he forced us to be the mainstream that was missing from his screenplay. He was showing us the street hustlers and power players, the porn shops and upholstered offices, as if we were in his movie, as if we were in the mid-sized sedans driving quickly past the boys partially hidden by awnings and parking meters. The middle class, as it almost always is with any kind of culture, is his intended viewer as well as his character stand-in. Our presence, as voyeurs and thinking, feeling participants, fills in the gaps. The missing character is us.

Gus Van Sant intentionally assigns us the most passive role and the least interesting one. We end the movie not wanting to be ensconced in the mainstream and therefore invisible to those who are really living, whose lives have the potential for great reward but also great failure. By the time the closing credits are rolling, we're frustrated with the mundane, and we want the different life, the risky one, the one we had just spent an hour and a half watching from the sidelines. The one that would be known throughout the 1990s as *alternative*.

MIKE AND SCOTT: QUEER OR NOT?

In 1991, everyone involved with *My Own Private Idaho* insisted that the film wasn't about being gay. "It's as much about gays as *Five Easy Pieces* is about oil-well diggers," River Phoenix claimed. At the time, the film's themes of queerness weren't discussed as much as its depictions of prostitution or homelessness or even narcolepsy. The unrequited love that Mike has for Scott was rarely defined as gay in reviews; instead, many of the critics wrote about the sweetness of their affection for each other, or about the comedy in their three-way sexual encounter with Hans in a Snake River hotel room. This seems like a purposeful omission; after all, River Phoenix and Keanu Reeves had been teen actors and were just starting their careers in adult roles. River's longtime agent, Iris Burton, who had been concerned about River's reputation, drug use, and drunk driving, said, after filming, "I never liked that fucking *My Own Private Idaho*. It should have stayed in the trash where it belonged." In 1991, it was still possible to keep the private lives of famous people relatively private, and one wonders if the teams of publicists and managers that surrounded both young actors were worried about their clients being labeled gay at a time when most gay actors were still deep in the closet. Sexuality, as it was more rigidly defined then, wasn't discussed in any depth in mainstream media. Two years later, when actor Will Smith refused to share an onscreen kiss with another male actor in *Six Degrees of Separation*, his decision was newsworthy but left unexamined by the mainstream media. Imagine the reaction on Twitter if a young actor with his level of fame did the same thing today.

In the years since 1991, there have been discussions in magazines and online about *My Own Private Idaho*'s influence on LGBTQ culture, my favourite being *Out*'s interview with Gus Van Sant, "The Enduring Power of *My Own Private Idaho*," which discusses Keanu's and River's status as celebrities, sexuality, and the impact of the film's visibility and wide distribution with New Line Cinema. However, there are questions the article doesn't raise that nagged fans and critics of *My Own Private Idaho* and New Queer Cinema scholars for years. Is it good or bad that Mike and Scott never actually identify as gay? What does it mean that the johns in the movie who pay for gay male sex are portrayed as comic or violent or sexually repellant? Does placing these young men on the streets and on the fringes of the mainstream mean that Gus Van Sant is marginalizing queerness?

In 1991, being a gay man was still intimately tangled with HIV/AIDS. *The Normal Heart*, the Tony Award–winning play by Larry Kramer, was first staged in New York in 1985. *Philadelphia*, the film that crystallized this crisis in the mainstream, would be released to great acclaim in 1993, the same year that *Angels in America*, written by Tony Kushner, won the Pulitzer. In the news, many of the narratives about being a gay man were grim news stories about men falling ill and dying, or about U.S. President Ronald Reagan refusing to acknowledge that an epidemic even existed. Popular media did a very good job of ignoring the plurality of queer narratives, and many people were still struggling with the definitions of gay, straight, and bi, never mind a spectrum of sexuality and gender.

For many, *My Own Private Idaho* was our first cultural experience with LGBTQ themes. *My So-Called Life*, featuring the gay character Rickie, was still three years away from its television premiere. By the time I watched *My Own Private Idaho* in the theater, I had only ever seen one queer character in mainstream media, and that was Glen, Snake's brother on *Degrassi Junior High*, who came out of the closet in an episode that aired in 1989. Even though Glen's sexuality was the plot point that this entire episode was developed around, the story was really Snake's, about how he would come to accept his brother's admission. Glen was just the gay brother. Snake was where our sympathies lay.

Queer stories had, of course, been present in American film for years, first as subtext or a series of innuendos in mainstream movies — think *Ben-Hur* (1959) or *Some Like it Hot* (1958) — and then as a movement of experimental art films in the late 1980s and early 1990s, termed the New Queer Cinema by critic B. Ruby Rich in 1992. Films such as Todd Haynes's *Poison* (1991) and Van Sant's *Mala Noche* (1985) are oft-cited examples. In between these two periods, there were a few other filmmakers who brought queerness to movie screens, sometimes explicitly and sometimes not: Andy Warhol and John Waters, for example, as well as Susan Seidelman, who directed the delightfully joyful *Desperately Seeking Susan* (1985), featuring the most compelling acting work of Madonna's career.

Mike and Scott, though, were the first characters I had ever seen who were young and unrepentantly sexually active. In his interview with *Out*, Gus Van Sant remarked, "I hear a lot of different stories like that from certain generations, this story about it being their first gay film. My former assistant was from Birmingham, Alabama, and he said he'd seen it there before he'd come out." Notably, Mike and Scott weren't burdened with secrets, but were openly living their lives as hustlers, in full view of everyone who happened to be around, including Scott's forbidding father. Their lives weren't easy; after all, they were still homeless, still working in the sex trade in often dangerous situations. But the moments of joy — pranks in a park late at night, motorcycle rides through the city, flying to Rome on a whim — were striking at a time when narratives of queer sexuality were often painful and about HIV/AIDS or coming out of the closet to parents who might disown you. *My Own Private Idaho* is frequently and refreshingly buoyant. There is a real sense of absurdity here, in almost every scene. *My Own Private Idaho* owes many of its lighter moments — Mike and Scott pretending to have noisy sex in front of Jack Favor's assistants, how the boys egging Bob Pigeon on while he's embellishing the story of the prank burglary — to Shakespearean slapstick comedy (tragedy's necessary counterpoint) and the ebullient gang of roughnecks in *Henry IV*.

The problematic question of whether *My Own Private Idaho* did enough in a political or social sense is tough to answer in 2017. Queerness had, for so long, existed in film on the fringes, either as hints in Hollywood movies, inserted by queer filmmakers, or as a theme in art films, which lacked wide distribution, a key point in 1991, when the only way to access a movie was if your local theater or video store decided to order it. Gus Van Sant himself said in an interview with *American Film* in 1991 that he had never thought of Mike and Scott as identifying as gay men, saying instead, "They're whatever

49

street hustlers are." He went on to explain that the position of the film itself, rather than the content, was a critical social statement, saying, "It's a political act to do a film like this." Like many artists, he preferred to place the emphasis on the trajectory of Mike and Scott's particular narrative, rather than picking apart that narrative for its politics.

However, the fact remains that the only characters in the film who admit to having specifically queer desires are the male johns, who are an exercise in eccentricity — they're sometimes creepy, sometimes clownish, and always presented to us as the opposite of sexually attractive, so much so that when Mike first meets Hans, the john who eventually pays for a three-some, he yells, "Why don't you go home? Go the fuck home!" The beautiful boys who fulfill these desires, on the other hand, are living on the streets, without enough money to pay anyone to do anything for them. They are sex workers without the polish and happy ending of Vivian in *Pretty Woman*, which had been released the year before, in 1990, and is perhaps the happiest, shiniest film version of sex work ever made. Mike and Scott are certainly beautiful, as Julia Roberts is in *Pretty Woman*, but Mike and Scott also bathe in public washrooms and sleep under piles of grubby blankets wherever they can. And their johns certainly don't look like Richard Gere.

None of the variations of queerness in *My Own Private Idaho* are normalized in the way that, say, *Will & Grace* would later normalize gay men for television viewers around the world. It can be easy to conclude that this only marginalizes queerness further, but I think that Gus Van Sant may have been making a different point altogether, which is that queerness had existed in the margins for a long time, and it was within those spaces, which, for many years, were invisible to the mainstream, that life happened. Just because his characters live on the street or pick up gay hustlers doesn't mean they don't create full lives for themselves away from heteronormative culture. The very opposite is true: they love, they fight, they do everything else humans do in that marginalized space, in their own fashion. In a way, this mirrors the evolution of New Queer Cinema, which developed on the outskirts of the cultural mainstream also, pushing cinematic and narrative boundaries as well as social ones. Like the characters in the films of Pedro Almodóvar and Donna Deitch, Mike and Scott grew their own stories on the fringes.

My Own Private Idaho, with its jerky cutaways and mannered dialogue, is in no way a realist film, and it could be argued that its lack of gritty details about sexuality shouldn't be viewed through a realist or political lens. But seeing sexuality in a film that is free of shame (there's disappointment and betrayal, but no shame) was a revolutionary experience for me, and for many other young viewers who had grown up with a lack of diversity, sexual or otherwise, in popular media.

Gus Van Sant made a very deliberate choice with his casting of River Phoenix and Keanu Reeves, especially for 1991: anyone could be gay. Your next door neighbor. Your teacher. Your aunt. Even the handsome boy actors whose faces were taped to the walls of your bedroom. Initially, Gus Van Sant considered casting Michael Parker and Rodney Harvey

(Digger and Gary in the film) in the lead roles, but it became clear that in order for *My Own Private Idaho* to work in wider release, River and Keanu were the more practical and commercial option. But their presence is also culturally significant, not just a ticket to secure financing, distribution, and an audience. The film was suggesting that anyone could be queer, yes, but it was also suggesting that queerness held social validity, that a story featuring queerness could attract big name, beautiful actors. And that their story, which is, at its core, about love and belonging, deserved as much consideration (and financing) as *City Slickers* or *Hudson Hawk*.

When I watch *My Own Private Idaho* now, its discussion of queer sexuality seems sweetly naïve, particularly in the porn shop scene early on in the movie. Mike and Scott and their group of friends are posed on the covers of gay porn magazines and talk to each other from their respective shelves at the store. The visual is reminiscent of the opening sequence to *The Brady Bunch*, when all the members of the family are interacting from their squares in a grid. Here, the young men are all shirtless and pouting at the camera, except for Mike, who is on a cross, his head hanging, a sexy, gay Christ figure (fitting, given that he is the one who, by the end of the film, sacrifices the most: he loses both Scott and his mother). Scott, wearing a cowboy hat, says to the camera, "I'll sell my ass. I do it on the street occasionally for cash. Or I'll be on the cover of a book. It's when you start doing things for free that you start to grow wings . . . You grow wings and become a fairy." His theory on being gay — that men can have sex with each other but can't really love each other

— sounds quaint, a way of ordering sexuality so that his own behaviour follows a trajectory that makes sense to him. This film, of course, was released more than a quarter century ago, and Gus Van Sant, in writing that scene, shows us how queerness was discussed and practiced in the mainstream at that time. Living queer experiences, as Mike and Scott do, was an act of subversion already, and it seems inevitable that the theories of sexuality that they could articulate would be more unformed than their actual decisions and actions.

IT'S RAINING MEN

My Own Private Idaho is a relentlessly masculine film. Although women are a part of Bob Pigeon's loose gang of young people, only two female characters speak: the wealthy older woman who picks up Mike, Scott, and Gary and drives them back to her big house in her fancy car, and Carmella, who mostly speaks Italian. For a long time, I worried about the Gus Van Sant's choice to include almost no women in his breakout film. Women, of course, play pivotal roles in *Drugstore Cowboy*, especially Kelly Lynch, whose portrayal of Dianne provides the story with an earthy, realist cynicism, a direct counterpoint to Matt Dillon's earnest and twitchy boy-man. In *My Own Private Idaho*, however, both the older woman and Carmella spend most of their screen time gazing at Mike or Scott, their onscreen existence defined solely by their relationships with these two men. For female viewers, this can be problematic.

However, the lack of women doesn't necessarily mean a lack of a gendered spectrum.

Masculinity is expressed in multiple ways in *My Own Private Idaho*: Bob Pigeon, the stand-in, gay, father figure; Mike, the man-child who gives his heart away to another man; Jack Favor, the imperious politician whose physical dominance is softened by his wheelchair; Digger, the soft-spoken hustler with the smooth face and harrowing first date story; Scott, the swaggering, cocky bro, who plans only for himself. The men in *My Own Private Idaho* are nurturing or buffoonish or quiet. When committing a robbery in the middle of the night, they wear bright pink bathrobes, a kind of Barbie-at-the-spa-meets-Jesuit-priest aesthetic. Gus Van Sant, instead of giving us men and women, has given us a range of masculinity, where men are allowed to have sex with other men or women, where power and victimhood can co-exist within the same character.

The idea of gender as a separate entity from sex or sexuality was not new in 1991 and had been discussed at length in the groundbreaking book *Gender Trouble* by Judith Butler, but it certainly wasn't mainstream either. Until 2013, the *Diagnostic and Statistical Manual of Mental Disorders* still listed the experience of being transgender as Gender Identity Disorder, essentially pathologizing it in medical terms. Expressions along the gender spectrum were sometimes visible in popular culture — think Marlene Dietrich in *Morocco*, Dustin Hoffman in *Tootsie*, Boy George in Culture Club videos — but they certainly weren't the men and women whom we saw most often in the media. *My Own Private Idaho* is an entire world of men who don't always "act like men." Mike and Scott aren't Arnold Schwarzenegger and Sylvester Stallone. Bob Pigeon isn't a jolly, benevolent patriarch like Tim Allen (although, in fairness, both are versions of Shakespeare's bumbling fools). It's a world where men are tops or bottoms, depending on the day, and where they wear flashy new clothes bought by a sugar daddy. They are douchebags and con artists, lovers and politicians, caregivers and philanderers. Gus Van Sant may have omitted women from his movie, but in their place he presented us with a range of masculinity, a kind of conversation about what men are, in opposition to what they are expected to be.

THE CULTURAL MESSENGER

My Own Private Idaho gave us a reason to talk about life on the margins by bringing that life into the mainstream, in the most visible way possible: a movie in commercial release starring two of the most popular young actors of the early 1990s. It put sex work, homelessness, and queerness on screens around the world and made being alternative look and sound beautiful, romantic, and exciting. *My Own Private Idaho* didn't create the margins; the margins had always existed, in varying forms. But what it, along with Nirvana and Douglas Coupland, did was bring the margins into the mainstream just enough so that it seemed interesting, adventurous, and, above all else, desirable. In the process, the mainstream became far more polymathic, resulting in the kind of cultural discussions we have today about, for example, the television series *Black-ish*, which airs on ABC, a major (and mainstream) network. There is a pivotal role for these sorts of cultural messengers, figures like Madonna (who brought early 1980s gay nightclub culture to the masses), the Beastie Boys (who made rap accessible to white kids living in the suburbs), and Ellen DeGeneres (who played a huge role in the wide acceptance of queerness in North America). The art and entertainment they created may not have been new, and they may have been appropriating and commodifying culture that had grown in marginalized spaces in spite of and often in protest to oppression, but the fact remains that they brought that culture to everyone else. And in doing so, they gave that marginalized culture a bigger audience and a more visible position within the mainstream, even if that position was riddled with problematic questions of identity and colonialism. This cultural messenger role is, however, relevant for *My Own Private Idaho*. It brought a particular version of *alternative* (or grunge, if you will) to the rest of us, and soon enough we all wanted to buy in. Within five years, many of us wore the thrift store clothes, pierced our eyebrows, took ecstasy, and danced at clubs with no names. We didn't know if we were changing the world, but we knew that the world that had come before — the polished pop music and slick movies — wasn't the kind of world we wanted to live in. At least, not anymore.

4

The Medium Is the Message

I NEVER THOUGHT I COULD BE A REAL MODEL

In a conversation about Sinead O'Connor with Scott and another hustler, Mike — that beautiful, broken drifter — says, without emotion, "I've never been to a concert." This small piece of dialogue lands quietly. No one in the film reacts to it. There is only a heartbeat of subsequent silence.

Mike is the ultimate outsider. Even among the gang of boys that hitchhikes from Seattle to Portland and back again, he is the one who has the most to forget. He was a feral child. He is and acts like a feral adult or, really, a bigger feral child, falling into narcoleptic sleep after spasms that are ungainly and violent, a dance performed by an untrained, uninhibited dancer. Unlike Scott, there is no rich father waiting for him.

Unlike Scott, he has never been to a concert, only traveled on roads that, in his words, look like a "fucked-up face."

Mike is the one we're supposed to love. He remains loyal to Bob. He is open, hiding nothing from Scott, not even feelings that he knows will never be returned. In the last scene, his bag and shoes are stolen, and we want to cry and laugh at the same time. Scott betrays him and elicits our hatred. It's the oddly steadfast Mike, with his double status as the Other, whom we want to be. River Phoenix was 20 when *My Own Private Idaho* began filming and, in some shots, reads much younger, his skin spotted with acne and his voice cracking with emotion during the confessional campfire scene with Keanu Reeves. In many ways, this film is a classic a coming-of-age story.

THIS ROAD NEVER ENDS

Mike's childhood flickers at the edges of *My Own Private Idaho*. The home movie–style footage, featuring an infant Mike, his older brother, and his mother dressed in white, always laughing, sometimes dancing, bubbles up whenever Mike remembers his mother unexpectedly — on the street or during a date. He longs for his mother, examining a postcard she sent his brother, looking for clues as he travels to Idaho and Italy. Although *My Own Private Idaho* isn't about Mike's childhood, it's his childhood that drives this very adult story forward or, rather, in a complete circle.

Mike travels on that road in Idaho three times: the film

begins and ends with him standing in the sunshine, looking down the asphalt for a car or a bike or a rabbit. But he also travels there in the middle of the movie with Scott to visit his older brother, the one person who might know where Mike's mother is or what her real story might be. Idaho is where Mike speaks out loud the deepest secrets of his past and present: alone with Scott at a campfire in the middle of the bush, he tells him he loves him; goaded by his brother, he admits that he knows his brother is also his father. In Seattle and Portland, where Mike is one of many hustlers looking for a john, his childhood and the deep hurts about neglect and incest and mental illness are kept at bay. He's just another lost young man wandering through the shadows, concerned with the present: money, food, shelter. His past can be forgotten, except when he has a narcoleptic fit.

Mike, who is an open, restless hero, knows that he needs to find his mother, or at least the version of his mother who says gently during one of his flashbacks, "I know you're sorry." Mike, as a streetwise hustler, must know that his mother, even if he were to find her, may not be the loving vision in white he sees in his sleep. After all, his mother's presence in his life has so far been characterized by her absence. And yet, he goes back to Idaho to find her, to that same road and same place where everything he feels and knows comes to light.

Sometimes, coming-of-age stories are about shaking off the past, leaving behind a painful early life that feels like a dead weight. Think of films like *Double Happiness* by Mina Shum or *Dead Poets Society*, directed by Peter Weir. *My Own*

Private Idaho, though, is not so linear. Mike's flashbacks arrive and recede. His life on the street, even after his heart is broken and Bob Pigeon dies, never really changes. He still sleeps on sidewalks (sometimes passed out from narcolepsy, sometimes purposefully) and still goes on dates for money. At the end, when Mike is standing on the side of that same road, he says, "This road never ends. It probably goes all around the world," before passing out one last time. Rather than moving away from Mike's past, Gus Van Sant's narrative choices suggest that Mike's coming-of-age story is about revisiting his past and then giving it space in his present life. When Scott is at his father's funeral, and the rest of his hustler friends are at Bob's wake down the hill, Mike looks back at Scott with a defiant expression on his face. He's not the one who has anything to be ashamed of, and he's not the one who has run away from anything. This scene, where Mike jumps on his fellow mourners (most notably Budd, played by Flea, whose grief is violent, sad, and comic) and howls into the sky in full view of the entire Favor family, is Mike's way of showing Scott that he is emotionally whole, a product of his childhood, adolescence, and nascent adulthood. Mike never leaves anyone or any memory behind. He would rather carry them all with him.

CULTURAL DECENTRALIZATION

Whenever I think of Gus Van Sant's storytelling, I always think that the apparent story is never the real story. He can be reticent in interviews, usually preferring to discuss the film and the characters without going deeper into what all of it means in a larger social or cultural or even personal context. In a 1991 article for *Interview*, River Phoenix played the role of journalist and asked Van Sant a series of questions about his work and artistic practice. In response to a question about identity, Van Sant said, "Yeah, I'm pretty much in the dark about myself." It's hard to know if this is a purposeful omission, or if he really doesn't know about his own motivations and psychology. But if we look at the structure of *My Own Private Idaho*, it's possible to see what Gus Van Sant might be saying about the experience of being human.

There are many elements in *My Own Private Idaho*: a big cast, a hero who is haunted by his past, urban and rural landscapes. Sometimes the shots are cut together in a way that defies chronology and place. The film is bright with colors that flash and flicker. Music, most notably "America the Beautiful" and "The Old Main Drag" by The Pogues, plays at surprising times and often not at all. And yet all of these elements come together to tell a story about Mike, a young man who is struggling to move forward when he constantly feels the pull of the past.

Stories are our way of making sense of our lives. Everybody's life is a series of events, some related, some not, and it's up to us, the protagonists in our own narratives, to impose an order or to create a structure that helps us understand the decisions we make and the pasts we leave behind. For people who live in the margins, like Mike and Scott and, to a degree, Gus Van Sant, who has been openly gay for his entire film career, this is a particularly important practice. If your life has been marked by familial rifts, exclusion, and, perhaps, violence, accepting the ways in which these traumas have changed you is necessary to survival. Building a story, one where you are the central character, is a powerful political act and is doubled if and when that story is disseminated. *My Own Private Idaho*, the sometimes messy movie that is really a deliberate synthesis, can be viewed as just this kind of act. Mike is a marginalized drifter who has never owned anything in his life. He bounces from odd experience to the next odd experience. And yet it is *his* story that Gus Van Sant has chosen to tell. If Mike's fragmented life is important enough to warrant a cohesive movie, then so is yours.

5

The Afterlife of Mike and Scott

BUILDING OUR ADULT LIVES

In two different scenes, Mike and Scott and their friends, all outcasts from previous lives, gather in a Chinese diner in Portland. They eat, talk, smoke, and comfort each other after long nights hustling on the street, after disappointments or heartbreak, after the world outside has become far too much. They're like a herd of starlings coming together, huddled for whatever measure of affection they can give or receive. In the absence of a student pub at a university, or a water cooler in an office, the young men and women in *My Own Private Idaho* gather here.

The Chinese restaurant is a microcosm, both of the movie and of the world in which the movie played an influential cultural role. Mike, Scott, and Bob Pigeon, exiled by their families and friends, create their own community, one in which plans are never long-term and oddities — like being the aging, decrepit leader of a gang of homeless youth — are celebrated. The restaurant is where Mike and Scott are fed, get warm, and sometimes fall asleep. In this relative comfort, the real stories — sometimes funny, sometimes violent, always emotionally complex — are told. Even in the abandoned hotel, there is a level of artifice or façade; it's at the hotel that Bob speaks his most florid Shakespearean lines and where Mike and Scott's idea for a prank is hatched. It's the diner where the boys and girls feel safest and are at their most unguarded.

After grunge came and went, at the end of the 1990s, there was an empty space for how people could identify themselves or form a community, youth who'd come of age with grunge and couldn't align themselves with the mainstream and who still felt a connection to the idea of *alternative*. Realistically, as we were heading into adulthood, we couldn't attend music festival after music festival with our glow sticks and clove cigarettes, and most of us didn't want to. We were starting to get married, look for homes, consider having children. Most of us still didn't have traditional jobs or careers. Or, if we did, we were building those careers in new ways, by creating our own tech start-up companies or self-publishing our science fiction novels. And we were also looking for ways to make our adult lives meaningful. After all, having spent our adolescence beating at the perfect, manicured world that mainstream 1990s culture was all about, we weren't likely to accept a trajectory that skimmed the surface of politics or gender or social justice. We had grown used to looking for music or art or books in unexpected places — dive bars, zines, open mics. Why should our relationship with the greater world be any different?

Many people of my generation, who had once jumped with abandon in the mosh pit at a Pearl Jam concert, actively looked for community outside of our jobs, for places we could create or play or love. We took to the internet and found our tribes, whether they were people who wanted to brew their own beer, or people who dressed like stuffed animals, or people who wrote themselves into *Harry Potter* fan fiction. The mainstream began to fall apart as we rushed for the edges and made our own circles of culture and interests and relationships. Perhaps the ultimate goal was to find people we loved being with and work that we loved doing, and to turn both of those things into paying jobs and long-term relationships, but we always knew that we might never accomplish this. We might be running a slam poetry festival without drawing a salary for two or five or ten years. We might never find a partner to build a home and a family with. But we took the risk anyway.

We became polyamorous, diversified, jacks-of-all-trades. If we couldn't find it, we made it.

We were abandoning the mainstream and, without us, the mainstream (on shaky ground as it was) began to split apart. From the early 2000s onward, most of us were creating communities without even thinking about how all of these different groups formed on different interests would affect the older, more traditional ways of building careers and relationships. But, as it turns out, our drive to find meaning outside of a nine-to-five job and a monogamous, lifelong marriage changed how we made decisions for the years to come.

WE DON'T WANT TO BE PERFECT ANYMORE

In an early scene, Mike is shivering on the street, waiting for a potential john to pick him up. A luxury sedan slows down, and inside, a woman with polished makeup and a fur coat smiles at Mike through the open passenger window. Even in the dim light, her perfection is obvious, and Mike mutters to himself, "This chick's living in a new car ad." She is one of only two women in *My Own Private Idaho* who speaks, and her lines are opaque; she directs the young men waiting for her to have drinks in the kitchen and responds to Mike's disbelief that this beautiful woman has picked him up. In these lines, we have no idea what her story really is, what her kinks are, or how she spends her days. Her façade of perfection is smooth.

However, if we look closer at this scene in her big, opulently decorated house, we see that the façade isn't quite as glossy as it seems. She needs three male sex workers to get off. When Mike collapses in front of her, instead of seeming genuinely concerned, she touches him hesitantly and whispers, "Oh, shit." By the end of the scene, the other two young men are dragging Mike through the dark residential streets, quietly and quickly removing him from her house. His body, grubby and unconscious, lies on a grassy hill, a boxy mansion in the background.

Even when Gus Van Sant presents us with beauty or apparent perfection, like this highly mannered, wealthy woman, he can't resist cracking it open, just a little bit, to show us that multiplicity and opposition exist everywhere, that there are real human emotions behind every decision and every moment, small or big. And this idea — that nothing is ever as perfect as it seems, and we shouldn't want or expect perfection anyway — has characterized the decentralized world we now live in.

In the early 1990s, culture and products were brands in the true sense of the word. Nothing came to us that wasn't market-tested and beautifully packaged, whether that was a television show or a soft drink. It was during this time that television commercials, easily the most produced, edited, and carefully vetted advertising medium, had the most impact. Cindy Crawford, once one of the most visible models in the world, starred in a wildly popular Pepsi commercial, which aired during the Super Bowl in 1992. After *My Own Private Idaho*, Nirvana, and other innovators broke through the slickly produced cultural landscape, we saw an evolution in how products — cultural or otherwise — were presented to us. Janet Jackson evolved from the precise beat and choreography in *Rhythm Nation 1814* in 1989 to the looser, more fluid feel of *janet.* in 1993. By then, what Jackson and her team understood was that not even the mainstream music fan wanted a perfect pop spectacle anymore.

This change in cultural sensibility had its parallels in the wider world. Bigger companies downsized. Smaller companies — more mobile and responsive — began developing products like gourmet ice cream and organic beauty products in small, highly coveted batches. Self-publishing books became a viable reality for authors who had been overlooked at traditional publishing houses. Online dating sites refined their mission statements, and soon there were different sites for people looking for specific kinds of partners and relationships. And sexuality and gender were soon being considered as a spectrum, to allow for the plurality of human identity. It seemed that the mainstream was splintering into smaller pockets, or that the margins were becoming not so marginal, and that it was normal to have specific interests and do specific things, no matter how singular. The gloss and cultural imperialism of the 1980s had given way to multiplicity. *My Own Private Idaho* was a film that was released more widely than most independents and had a much bigger audience than either of Gus Van Sant's previous movies, and its narrative desire to break through the polished surface of things to access emotions or truths that Scott's father would call unseemly is part of its effect on the culture of the 1990s and beyond.

MIKE AND SCOTT IN THE NEW MILLENNIUM

When *My Own Private Idaho* was released, the critics loved it and responded positively to Gus Van Sant's vision. Roger Ebert wrote, "The achievement of this film is that it wants to evoke that state of drifting need, and it does. There is no mechanical plot that has to grind to a Hollywood conclusion, and no contrived test for the heroes to pass; this is a movie about two particular young men, and how they pass their lives." River Phoenix won acting awards for his role from the Venice Film Festival, the National Society of Film Critics, and the Independent Spirit Awards. Reviewers called it "a perfect synthesis" and "wholly original, wholly fresh." Keanu Reeves and River Phoenix were the cover feature in *Interview* and photographed for *Rolling Stone*. It gave both of them an identity beyond the mainstream Hollywood movies they had grown up acting in, and also gave them enough street cred that, in an interview, River could say, "I get negative shit all the time. I don't care."

Both actors, and especially River Phoenix, had made good films with good performances, but none of their previous roles had pushed at as many social and creative boundaries as *My Own Private Idaho*, which landed with critical praise and kicked the rest of us in the ass. The film — fragmented and saturated with color and dirt and a painfully beautiful masculinity — crept its way into popular culture and media, and its influence on artists who came of age in the 1990s can still be traced. James Franco, the ubiquitous actor, author, and professor, made a companion, semi-documentary film called *My Own Private River* in 2012 (the film played at festivals but never had a commercial release), citing his friendship with Gus Van Sant and his obsession with River Phoenix and the original film as the impetus behind the project. Franco's documentary, constructed mainly with outtakes supplied by Gus Van Sant, is by far the most directly inspired, but there are other, more meandering trails of influence.

My Body Is Yours, the excellent memoir by Michael V. Smith, explores his relationship with his father and, by extension, his relationship with masculinity. As a gay man, and one who never felt comfortable with the rigidity of traditional masculinity, he traces the trajectory of his life from childhood to middle age, and his growing realization that his identity as a man isn't dependent on what his father or the world has shown him. Gender, he learns, is whatever we are, in whatever form we want or need to take. *My Body Is Yours* circles around the genderqueer spectrum and the ways in which we construct sexual identity. Michael V. Smith, like me and other writers such as Zoe Whittall and Billeh Nickerson, came of age in the 1990s. The seeds of what we were going to write about — our relationships with our bodies, the ways in which sexuality bleeds into every component of our lives — were partially planted by popular culture in the 1990s. And for me and many others, that meant *My Own Private Idaho*.

The film's influence was not restricted to gender. Its lo-fi fragmentation, with abrupt cuts to brightly colored titles and shots of exploding barns, as well as lines of Shakespearean dialogue, is a particularly postmodern, 1990s structure. The story of Mike and Scott is straightforward enough at its core: two young street hustlers take to the road to understand their origins and also their futures. It is the extras, such as the scene with a numbers-obsessed john commanding Mike to scrub the furniture while he dances in joy on a spotless rug, like an absurdly intense Fred Astaire, that make the narrative of *My Own Private Idaho* something extraordinary. Gus Van Sant's editing choices can seem superficially haphazard, but each jerky cut to a shot of spawning salmon or still-life sex scene serves a purpose, and is a commentary on the ways in which we experience sensation in real time, as episodes rather than a seamless, progressive narrative, or how our understanding of our lives is built on a million different and seemingly unrelated events. This postmodern perspective has been part of story-telling for a long time (Laurence Sterne, James Joyce, *Bonnie and Clyde*), but during the 1990s and beyond, there has been a particular upswell of mainstream artists creating culture that pulls influence from the classic to the contemporary, from the stages to the streets, from canonical stories to immigrant ones: Junot Díaz, Zadie Smith, David Mitchell. The film-makers Paul Thomas Anderson and Spike Jonze. The fashion designer Giles Deacon. The pop singer Rihanna. Gus Van Sant, in *My Own Private Idaho*, was one of the first structural and visual magpies of the 1990s. Perhaps the best example of this eclectic assimilation is his use of *Henry IV*.

There is a lot of binary opposition in Shakespearean plays: Montague and Capulet, gravediggers and the Prince of Denmark, principled Othello and scheming Iago. *Henry IV* is no different with its dialectic drunken louts and royal intrigue. However, unlike many of the other plays, *Henry IV*'s main character, Prince Hal, who is the future King of England, moves effortlessly between the two worlds. He drinks with Falstaff and the other ruffians while he makes plans to return to the court and assume his responsibilities as the heir to the throne. High and low culture are distinct and polar in *Henry*

IV, but what isn't distinct is Prince Hal's real identity. He's not a character like Viola in *Twelfth Night*, who dresses like a boy to hide herself, with her class and gender fluidity structured as a plot point and visible to the audience. Hal never hides, but it's a mystery where his true loyalties lie. Is he a hoodlum at heart? Or is he slumming it in the taverns for temporary fun?

In *My Own Private Idaho*, Scott is Hal's parallel character, his father the powerful mayor of Portland rather than the King of England. Scott spends years living as a hustler and learning from (and teasing) Bob Pigeon. And he eventually returns to his family when his father dies, taking on his political legacy while betraying Bob and Mike. In a late scene with dialogue from *Henry IV, Part Two*, Scott stands in a high-end restaurant and refuses to face his old friends, who have asked him to honor his promise to employ them now that he has returned to his familial and moneyed responsibilities. Bob and Mike are forcibly removed by Scott's security (who were once his father's security), and the two worlds of political power and street hustling are separate once again, with no middle class to bridge the gap.

What makes Gus Van Sant's use of Prince Hal's narrative so postmodern is how it's inserted into *My Own Private Idaho* without introduction or explanation. Scott speaks lines inspired by Hal to a sleeping Mike on a lawn in Seattle after a failed night of sex work. Bob sees a friend in a Michael Jackson–esque leather jacket and mocks him with Shakespearean dialogue. While Keanu speaks his Shakespearean lines with a stagelike formality (as do Bob and Budd), River, whose lines are mostly contemporary, speaks with an unmistakable 1990s casualness. Gus Van Sant, who has said in interviews that this difference in delivery wasn't intentional, but that he liked the dialectic, is asking us, as an audience, to accept this jarring, verbal fragmentation, in the same way that he asks us to accept his visual fragmentation: the images of spawning salmon; the homes of Mike and Scott's johns, each one more oddly decorated than the last; Mike dressed as the mascot for Dutch Boy cleaner. Even the very foundation of the film itself is part of this fragmented, high-low tension: *My Own Private Idaho* is an independent art film (more of an anomaly in 1991 than it is today) and the very presence of actors like Keanu Reeves and River Phoenix is a cultural and structural mashup. Seeing the young Indiana Jones have sex with the time-traveling Ted was, at the very least, a surprise. Taken as a whole, Gus Van Sant seems to be telling us that humanity is everywhere: in high culture and low culture, in boardrooms and abandoned hotels, in the tragedy and comedy of Shakespeare. After all, the characters of *My Own Private Idaho* exist in worlds most of the audience will never experience. Most of us aren't high-powered politicians or street hustlers. But, just the same, the emotions those in the middle all understand — joy, despair, loneliness, love — proliferate in the high and the low.

My Own Private Idaho's combination of disparate influences is part of the postmodernity that marks the cultural output of my generation of artists. The idea of separate high and low cultures has, today, largely dissipated, a relic of the way our parents viewed Wagner versus Sir Mix-a-Lot. As a teenager, how many times did I hear my parents and friends' parents claim that rap wasn't music or that comic books weren't literature? Now, we write think-pieces on the feminism of the relentlessly popular Beyoncé and Taylor Swift, and buy the fashion collaborations of high-street retailers and luxury designers. We eat hot dogs with as much pleasure as lobster bisque. We use social media as a political protest tool. And we write books about movies that combined art with absurdity, *Henry IV* with BDSM. *My Own Private Idaho* was positioned at the very beginning of this multi-influenced way of learning and communicating about the world.

What we had learned from Mike and Scott and their gang of self-guided boys was a pivotal part of what we needed to feel creative and, essentially, human: building a center when we were the other, searching for purpose when purpose didn't come to us, ignoring the demographers who tried to define us, and using everything we had ever seen or watched or worn to explain what our world was becoming. When the old signifiers of successful humanity — marriage, career, stability — had already rusted over, this was how we reshaped our intimate relationships, our ways of disseminating and collecting information, our jobs, and, well, everything else in between.

WHAT'S EATING GUS VAN SANT?

While researching this book in the summer of 2016, I searched for Gus Van Sant on IMDb.com, and this is what I found: 25

producing credits, 35 directing credits, and 12 writing credits. He has directed, written, or produced feature and short films, documentaries, television series, and music videos (for the Red Hot Chili Peppers and David Bowie). His feature films are sometimes small (*Elephant*, *Mala Noche*) and sometimes hugely successful (*Good Will Hunting*, *Milk*). They can be almost inaccessibly odd (*Even Cowgirls Get the Blues*) or follow a deeply traditional narrative (*Finding Forrester*). A 2004 profile published in the *Guardian* opens with "This is the conspiracy theory doing the rounds — there are two Gus Van Sants. One makes inspired indie movies and is loved by true cineastes; the other is a mercenary who churns out Hollywood schmaltz-busters." His career, particularly after *My Own Private Idaho*, can seem haphazard or inexplicable, but there is consistency in the inconsistent, or a constant thematic thread that ties all of his work together, which is this: Gus Van Sant likes his misfits.

Good Will Hunting, which won Academy Awards in 1998 for its screenplay and for Robin Williams's performance as the kindly, bearded psychologist, is by far Gus Van Sant's most successful film. It launched the careers of Ben Affleck and Matt Damon, who wrote the script and acted in the lead roles, and cemented Robin Williams's reputation as a serious, dramatic actor. It's a straightforward movie with a linear plot: a janitor at M.I.T. is an undiscovered math genius who struggles with reconciling the beginnings of his academic life and his working-class, violent past.

Will is the ultimate misfit. Unlike Scott in *My Own Private Idaho*, who moves from the street and then back to city hall with relative ease, Will isn't comfortable anywhere. His familiar working-class life is fine, but even before anyone knows he has a formidable talent in mathematics, he spends his free time reading library books on every subject imaginable, a pastime that his friends admire but also find incomprehensible. When he is presented with opportunities to study and work in the field he loves, he sabotages them, running back to his construction-site and pub-drinking life, where his failure as a genius is just one item on a long list of disappointments for a young man whose ambitions are bordered on all sides by class barriers. He is wrapped up in painful memories: his parents' deaths, a foster father who beat him, prison. He socially insulates himself because that's easier than heartbreak or violence.

As I noted in chapter one, from his first film, *Mala Noche*, Gus Van Sant has used young male actors whose faces and bodies are visually riveting, and Matt Damon in *Good Will Hunting* is one of them. As Simon Hattenstone wrote in the *Guardian*, "They don't quite belong anywhere, because society deems them surplus to its needs." His films "are about young men struggling towards an identity," whether they're frustrated math prodigies living in South Boston, or heroin addicts robbing pharmacies, or hustlers living on the streets of Portland. Their beauty is a human touchstone. We all love watching beautiful people who present to us a kind of superhumanity; we gravitate to and feel more for people we find attractive, even if their appearance can seem unattainable. Why else do we take lifestyle advice from actors like Gwyneth

Paltrow and Jessica Alba, instead of from therapists or parenting coaches?

Our connection to beauty is universal, as is our search for identity. We all wander through life, looking for ways to define ourselves and become the people who drive our own narratives instead of the ones who have our narratives forced upon us. All of Gus Van Sant's heroes are misfits fighting through expectations and disappointments in order to figure out who they are or should be, and, looking at the trajectory of his career after 1991, it's easy to conclude that Gus Van Sant has been embroiled in his own identity journey. His filmography, which can seem random, makes a chaotic kind of sense.

The postmodern narrative and visual fragmentation in *My Own Private Idaho* and *Drugstore Cowboy* seem to apply in a funny, life-imitates-art way whenever I look at Gus Van Sant's history of filmmaking. Yes, all of his films explore the themes of belonging and exile (self-imposed or otherwise), but his magpie personality emerges when we look at his stylistic choices for each one of his features. *Mala Noche* is shaky and filmed very much like the home movies inserted into *My Own Private Idaho* — often out of focus, disconcertingly soundtrack-less in dramatic moments. *To Die For* is underground Hollywood noir, dark and moody and suffused with sexual longing. *Finding Forrester* stars Sean Connery, a.k.a. James Bond. *Psycho* is a shot-by-shot remake of the original film by Alfred Hitchcock. And *Milk* is a linear political biopic of Harvey Milk, the first openly gay man elected to public office in California.

Gus Van Sant, born in 1952, grew up, like most of us, in a world where television, newspapers, magazines, and radio were everywhere — at home, at school, in storefronts in every town and city in North America. Access to variety shows, comic strips, and mainstream movies was easy, if you had enough money to buy it. Gus Van Sant is also highly educated and a graduate of the Rhode Island School of Design. It's no surprise, then, that he became an artist who takes influence from everywhere, from every cultural medium he consumed from childhood onward. His creativity was formed from both the popular culture around him (he collects guitars and has a well-documented relationship with rock stars and their music, in particular David Byrne and Flea) and the more classic world of art school and art history. His work has always been an exercise in opposition, in creating a sense of discomfort in order to make his viewers pay attention. In a sense, this is how he's structured his filmmaking career: his choices can be read as deliberate, as exploring the poles of art films and Hollywood to keep, perhaps, his own creativity fresh. He has said, "I became involved in the mainstream partly because I thought, in order to affect change, you needed to be able to do it." But he has also said, "*Good Will Hunting* and *Finding Forrester* was like me going back, or trying to, in sentimental movie fashion, going back to make popular art, art for the populace." Moviemaking, for Gus Van Sant, is often about changing popular culture by inserting a subversive subtext into a more palatable Hollywood format, but also about paying homage to the popular culture that has shaped him and everyone else. Every artist, from

Warhol to Picasso to Linda Perry, exists in a cultural space between what is mainstream and what is marginal. There are always competing desires at work: to be as creatively free as possible and to also be mainstream enough to make a decent living (a tension that is mirrored in *My Own Private Idaho*, with its boundary-pushing aesthetic and Hollywood cast). The magic happens when artists disseminate something that allows the mainstream to understand and be permanently changed by the marginal, like Marcel Duchamp's famous *Fountain* or *Giovanni's Room* by James Baldwin.

Gus Van Sant's career after *My Own Private Idaho*, then, is not so confounding as it can seem at first glance. His brain, it appears, gathers influence from high and low, the popular and the maligned, middle-class obsessions and art theory. It's a postmodern mashup, to be sure, but it's also an artist's attempt to make sense of and change the world at the same time. His creative identity is a kind of funhouse mirror: a self-constructed identity that uses the exploration of identity as its driving, universal theme. We are all products, he seems to be saying, of where we come from and what we've watched or read or listened to, but in this cultural wake, we are also trying to understand who we are as individuals. Gus Van Sant is no different. His filmography uses traditional storytelling tools (Shakespearean structures, Hollywood-sanctioned beauty) while breaking apart that very same traditional storytelling (placing his beautiful actors in distinctly ugly settings). He uses established tropes and upends them with sexuality or gender fluidity or jerky camera shots. He is defining his creative role by making films that are both who he was and who he might become or wishes he could be. And this, perhaps, has been Gus Van Sant's legacy for the 21st century world as we know it: we are constantly acknowledging our pasts, presents, and futures, no matter how mundane they seem, no matter how dysfunctional or weird we think they are. His films lead us to understand that this eclecticism — seen every single day during our interactions with the polymathic world — is still human, still relatable, and still beautiful.

Epilogue

It's ten o'clock on a Sunday night and I'm in bed, my laptop playing *My Own Private Idaho* one more time. By now, I've watched the movie more times than I can remember, and more often still as I've been writing this book and thinking about how Gus Van Sant changed and was emblematic of the 1990s and, subsequently, the years that followed. I'm 40 now, a single mother and a writer. My life is a patchwork of teaching and poetry and dog walks and freelancing. I had a real job once, ten years ago. My days are self-structured, built around the unpredictability of parenting a six-year-old and deadlines and student manuscripts. In the mid-1990s, I had pink pixie hair and opinions on everything, from politics to culture to publishing. Not much has changed, except the hair. And maybe some of my opinions. (Maybe.)

For years, the spectre of being alternative haunted me, even when grunge wasn't cool anymore. I knew, from 1991 onward, that my decisions were not always going to be traditional ones, or at least ones that made the most respectable sense. I dropped out of graduate school when I was 22. I got married at 24, even after my friends told me, repeatedly, that I was too young. I quit my real job at 29 to write full-time, and my agent worried that I would starve. My marriage ended at 38, and I decided to keep freelancing instead of looking for a steady job. None of these are shocking decisions in 2017, but it's precisely because of the social and cultural changes that occurred in the 1990s and beyond that these choices are, while still nontraditional, possible and possibly rewarding. It's because of the sea change that *My Own Private Idaho* helped spur in the mainstream that we can talk about gender as a spectrum, or that we encourage more plurality of voices in popular culture than we ever have before.

Watching *My Own Private Idaho* now can feel like nostalgia, as if what I'm watching is a quaint, old-fashioned portrayal of gender and sexuality and street-based adventure. After all, I'm a middle-aged mother now, and I've lived through relationships and heartbreak and the anxiety of not knowing what I want from love and intimacy, and I know things now that I had no way of understanding when I was 15. But this backward view is a flawed way of watching Mike and Scott. They exist only in this film in 1991. Their youth and that moment in time are tangled up together. Can you imagine them hustling on the street as 40-year-old men? Or leaving the streets and juggling mortgages and children and Little League schedules? Or checking their iPhones for an Uber driver when their motorcycle breaks down on that lonely stretch of road in the middle of Idaho? If the film's version of sexual emancipation and life on the margins seems sweetly naïve, that's our current 21st-century perspective coloring the past with our Twitter activism and intersectional politics and latest Tinder hook-up. Go back and read your adolescent diary. You'll see what I mean.

What occurs to me tonight, as I re-watch this movie that I know so well, is that we can be critical of Gus Van Sant's vision, but we also have to be aware that *My Own Private Idaho* is an essential link in a cultural chain of events that led to *Singles* and *Reality Bites* and *Swingers*, to Dan Savage and polyamory and internet pornography. To our discussions on whether Kim Kardashian is too sexual to be respectable or should be respected because of her overt sexuality. All of these cultural players reflect the evolution of our preoccupations and are reasons why Mike and Scott's story can seem cute or not subversive enough. But it is because of Mike and Scott and other parallel moments that we have even arrived at a cultural place where we have the tools to consider their story in these critical ways. *My Own Private Idaho* helped create the world we live in today, where we can discuss the complicated topics of human relationships with an openness that didn't exist before 1991.

I'm not suggesting, of course, that we can't be more open and more accepting of plurality. There is always more progress to be made and issues that we haven't even thought of yet. And there will be cultural moments that are happening right now that will resonate with us in 2043. Perhaps it will be how Beyoncé remade entertainment in her own image. Or how we find political community online and then feel safe enough to voice dissent. Or how sustainability is changing how we buy and eat. Maybe it will be these moments that will compel someone, 26 years younger than I am, to write a book.

It is because of *My Own Private Idaho* that I care about sexuality and cultural politics, that I became a writer who tries to challenge what we think about gender and bodies and navigating race. I may never have been a street hustler in Portland, and I may never have had a father who was mayor or a mother who was institutionalized, but I had a childhood that was also marked by traumas, some big and some small, and, every single day of my adolescence and young adulthood, I worried that I would never figure any of it out and that I was destined to be buried by confusion. Mike and Scott were the cinematic embodiments of this anxiety, the ones who felt so stifled by their lack of choices that they took to the streets, the wide open world of possibilities, to try everything at least once so that they could, one day, direct their lives in a way that felt fitting and individual. They started me on a life that has been defined by non-traditional choices and, right now, as I watch Mike for the last time on that fucked-up face of a road, I'm weirdly and steadfastly certain that all of my choices were the right ones.

*Sources

Butler, Judith. *Gender Trouble: Feminism and the Subversion of Identity*. New York: Routledge, 1990.

Coupland, Douglas. *Generation X: Tales for an Accelerated Culture*. New York: St. Martin's Griffin, 1991.

Diagnostic and Statistical Manual of Mental Disorders. 4th edition. Arlington: American Psychiatric Association, 1994.

Drugstore Cowboy, directed by Gus Van Sant. Avenue Pictures, 1989.

Ebert, Roger. "*My Own Private Idaho*," *Chicago Sun-Times*, October 18, 1991.

Edwards, Gavin. *Last Night at the Viper Room: River Phoenix and the Hollywood He Left Behind*. New York: It Books, 2013.

Foot, David K. Boom, *Bust & Echo: How to Profit from the Coming Demographic Shift*. Toronto: Macfarlane, Walter & Ross, 1997.

Good Will Hunting, directed by Gus Van Sant. Miramax, 1997.

"Gus Van Sant." IMDb.com. Accessed February 18, 2016.

Hattenstone, Simon. "All the World's an Art School," *Guardian*, January 24, 2004.

Howe, Desson. "*My Own Private Idaho*," *Washington Post*, October 18, 1991.

Kurt Cobain: Montage of Heck, directed by Brett Morgen. HBO Documentary Films, 2015.

Loud, Lance. "Shakespeare in Black Leather," *American Film*, September/October 1991.

Marin, Rick. "Grunge: A Success Story," *New York Times*, November 15, 1992.

My Own Private Idaho, directed by Gus Van Sant. Fine Line Features, 1991.

Phoenix, River. "My Director and I," *Interview*, March 1991.

Portwood, Jerry. "The Enduring Power of *My Own Private Idaho*," *Out*, October 25, 2015.

Rea, Stephen. "An Eye on the Private River Phoenix," *Philadelphia Inquirer*, October 13, 1991.

Rich, B. Ruby. *New Queer Cinema: The Director's Cut*. Durham: Duke University Press, 2013.

Shakespeare, William. *Henry IV, Part 1*. New York: Simon & Schuster, 2005.

Shakespeare, William. *Henry IV, Part 2*. New York: Simon & Schuster, 2005.

Smith, Michael V. *My Body Is Yours*. Vancouver: Arsenal Pulp, 2015.

Sykes, Gini and Paige Powell. "River and Keanu," *Interview*, November 1991.

Thelma & Louise, directed by Ridley Scott. Metro-Goldwyn-Mayer, 1991.

Top Gun, directed by Tony Scott. Paramount, 1986.

Acknowledgments

To Jen Knoch, Crissy Calhoun, Jack David, and everyone at ECW Press for challenging me to write in new forms.

To Carolyn Swayze, for never laughing when I tell her my book ideas.

To Sandra Ka Hon Chu, for accompanying me on this journey to Idaho and back.

To Shawn Krause and Andrea MacPherson, for reading drafts of this book and reassuring me I could actually write it.

To June Hutton and Mary Novik, for listening.

To my friends in the English Department at the University of the Fraser Valley, for giving me the time, space, and money to write this book.

To Andrew Chesham and Wayde Compton and everyone at The Writers' Studio at Simon Fraser University, for gainfully employing me so I can continue to write.

And, as always, to Oscar and Molly, the beating hearts of every book and my entire life.

Jen Sookfong Lee was born and raised in Vancouver's East Side, and she now lives with her son in North Burnaby. She is the author of *The Conjoined*; *The Better Mother*, a finalist for the City of Vancouver Book Award; *The End of East*; and *Shelter*, a novel for young adults. A popular CBC Radio One personality, Jen appears regularly as a contributor on *The Next Chapter* and is a frequent co-host of the *Studio One Book Club*.

Get the
eBook free!*

*proof of purchase
required

At ECW Press, we want you to enjoy this book in whatever
format you like, whenever you like. Leave your print book
at home and take the eBook to go! Purchase the print
edition and receive the eBook free. Just send an email to
ebook@ecwpress.com and include:

- the book title
- the name of the store where you purchased it
- your receipt number
- your preference of file type: PDF or ePub?

A real person will respond to your email with your eBook
attached. And thanks for supporting an independently
owned Canadian publisher with your purchase!